EMBEADERY

Using Classic Embroidery Stitches in Beadwork

Margaret Ball

INTRODUCTION

A love affair with beads

It started in the Paris Flea Market, in 1959. I was eleven years old. My mother had been teaching night school in the Blue Ridge mountains for three years to save up the money for a summer in England, and she was generous enough to take me with her – and even to give up a few precious days of her English holiday for us to go to Paris to let me practice my French on real live people. And, of course, I had to go to the Marche aux Puces...and I could have stayed there for a week, looking at little carved boxes and agate snuffboxes and green face-shaped beads and Chinese ivory carvings. But the thing I *had* to have was a scrap of bead embroidery on black net, probably the last remnants of some flapper's evening dress. It was about twice as big as a playing card, solidly worked in gold and red and blue bugle beads, and I poured it from one hand to the other like a fountain of liquid fireworks and loved the glitter and shimmer and drape of it.

That piece has not been part of my life for years – probably the net disintegrated from too much loving handling – but the love of beads and bead embroidery that began in the Marche aux Puces has been a lifelong companion.

Why I wrote this book

I started writing this book for a very simple reason: in years of doing bead embroidery I've worked out a lot of stitches and variations which just don't get described in the standard book on the subject. Anybody would think there was some law limiting bead embroiderers to couching, back stitch, seed stitch, and a few very tentative loops and fringes! As it happens, there's a great deal more you can do.

A *great* deal.

This was originally going to be one book containing Everything I Have To Say About Bead Embroidery.

Nup. Too much. When the section on embroidery-based stitches got to over 100 pages, I decided it was time to set it free as Book I. There will be more books covering raised work, fringes, beading with large and/or unconventional objects, preparing interesting backgrounds, embroidering three-dimensional forms, and incorporating bead embroidery into other art work. But this book is narrowly focused on taking a number of traditional embroidery stitches and showing how they can be adapted to beadwork.

Why do this? To add rhythm, texture, pattern, and excitement to your work – is that enough of a reason? To play with patterns and forms, seeing what happens when you interpret them rigidly and what happens when you let yourself go with the impulse of the moment? To do something with sequins besides making a bunch of little round sequin dots on fabric? To let the length and directional quality of bugle beads shine beside the roundness of rocailles, to set off those perfect pearls or crystals in frames of open chain stitch, to enrich your work with the intricate braided forms of beaded chain or herringbone stitch?

All right – I love beads. And sequins. And pearls and crystals and buttons and gemstone chips and just about anything else that will stand still and let me put a needle through it. And this book is for other people looking for ways to expand their love affair with beads, whether it's by making wonderful textured necklaces, or embellishing the seams of a crazy quilt block, or branching out into their own wild and wonderful beaded creations.

Embroidery-Based Stitches

Many of the stitches traditionally used by embroiderers can be adapted to bead work. In some ways we have less freedom in our stitching than if we were using embroidery thread, but in other ways we have exciting new possibilities.

The basic limitation is that a length of thread strung with beads isn't going to slide through fabric the way a length of embroidery thread does. This makes many of the looped and knotted stitches impossibly intricate (although we'll explore some ways of getting around that). The most important thing to be aware of here is that the number of beads you thread on for one stitch has to be just right, and that it varies depending on the type of stitch, the size of the bead, the area you're trying to cover and the stitch length that you are most comfortable with. In the stitch descriptions I'll recommend a specific number of seed beads to thread on, and indicate what size seed beads I'm using, but these numbers are just starting places. Even if you stay with the same exact size of beads, where I'm working with 10 Delicas per stitch you may feel more comfortable with 8 or 12 – a lot depends on the size of your hands, the thickness of the fabric you're using, whether you're working in a hoop or without one. It is <u>always</u> a good idea to work a small sample first, using the beads you plan to use and a comparable weight of base fabric, to make sure you know how many beads you want to string on with each stitch. A very small sample will suffice. But it's much better to put in five minutes making a sample than to plunge into a major work and later spend two hours picking out irregular stitches and removing seed beads from your lap.

To compensate for the recalcitrance of our "thread", we have an exciting freedom that also comes from the fact that each stitch is built out of beads on thread. In traditional embroidery, whatever thread you put on your needle, that's the color and texture of thread you'll be using until you thread a new needle. Even if you use a variegated thread, the way the variegations play out is determined by the colors on the thread and the thread usage of the stitch; you have little or no control. Thread embroiderers have to do contortions with two or even three needles at the same time to get something as simple as alternating colors.

We, on the other hand, have the freedom to redefine the color and texture of our "thread" each time we string a pinch of beads. Want to make every stitch a different color? Nothing to it – just line up your pots of beads and start sewing. Want to build color variations into the stitch itself, add big sparkly beads to emphasize a focal point or the end of a line, switch from matte to shiny texture and back again, gradually increase the size of beads so that a delicate line builds up to a thick cable? In bead embroidery we can do all that without ever changing the thread. As I discuss various stitches, I'll suggest ways these variations and others can be specially effective, but it's truly not possible to list every interesting thing you can ever do with a stitch. This book can be used as a reference guide to bead embroidery stitches; I hope you'll use it as more than that, as a set of jumping-off places that you can use as guidelines for discovering your own unique stitches, expressing your creative vision in your own way.

How to use this book

You could, if you're obsessive enough (and a lot of us beaders have a very strong obsessive-compulsive streak) start at the beginning and read straight through to the end, trying out every stitch and every variation.

If you're a free spirit who thinks that looking at the index is cheating, you could look at the color pictures, pick out something that appeals to you (like, say, the picture of open chain stitch with bugle beads and stars), turn to the page where instructions for that stitch appear, and start stitching.

I don't actually recommend this either; you'll probably get all frustrated and start mumbling, "What the #$($@ does she mean, TCT? What are all these parentheses about? Why didn't the damn woman explain how to hold your beads so that they end up looking like the diagram?"

What I'd recommend is this:

In Chapter 1, "The Basics," read the sections you need. If you're new to bead embroidery, read the first section, about materials to bead on and some general guidelines for choosing stitches. If you're familiar with beadwork but haven't embroidered much, take a look at the second section, where you'll find a quick overview of traditional embroidery and some recommended reading. If you know how to embroider but haven't done much with beads, read the third section for a discussion of beads, beading needles, and threads.

If you already know all that stuff, skip ahead to Chapter 2, on adapting embroidery stitches to beadwork. In this chapter I'll go over the three crossing techniques I've worked out and the simple notation I use for sequences of beads to be strung. This isn't rocket science, but the techniques and notation are going to come up again and again and again, so you might want to familiarize yourself with them before plunging into the book.

After that we're into the details of specific embroidery stitches. For each stitch I use the same general approach. First I describe ways of working the very basic stitch, with comments on which crossing techniques (if any are needed) work best for that stitch. This is covered in excruciating detail with diagrams that should guide you every step of the way; if they don't do that, then I haven't done my job.

After we get the basic form down, I start discussing variations, and here the level of detail changes somewhat. I don't like repeating the same exact instructions over and over again, any more than you like reading them, so I will say things like, "Work this exactly like the basic stitch until you get to this point, and then…." Sometimes there are variations on variations, and as we get farther and farther down the list the instructions are going to get briefer, sometimes as simple as "Do what you did before, only reverse the bead colors."

So, read and understand the basic crossing techniques. Have some scrap material and some beads handy. (Of course you're not going to pick triple color reverse herringbone with dangles for your first attempt, and do it on the wall quilt you're entering in Quilt National next week….right?) Pick a stitch and read the instructions for the basic form, maybe work a few samples, *then* go down into the variations. We'll all be much happier that way.

CHAPTER ONE: THE BASICS

All you need to make dazzlingly beautiful works of bead embroidery is a handful of beads, a beading needle, thread, and a firm fabric to apply the beads to. A pencil or, better, an erasable chalk marker, is helpful. And don't forget your sense of adventure!

What to bead on

You can apply bead embroidery to just about anything you can shove a needle through. But just like the rest of real life, some restrictions apply.

If you embroider on a very lightweight fabric, it'll be very hard to maintain the tension you need. The thread will slide back and forth through the fabric, the beads will flop this way and that, the embroidery will try to pucker here and sag there....and if this fabric is part of a garment, you can expect it to sag where the beads are applied. You *can* apply bead embroidery to clothes, but use common sense: expect to make a lot of stabilizing knots or back stitches, don't layer on the beads too heavily, stick with "safe" stitches like Extremely Secure Backstitch (see next chapter) rather than stitches involving 26-bead unanchored loops, and don't plan on throwing this garment into the washing machine.

If you embroider on a good thick piece of leather, the tension problem will solve itself and the beadwork will be stable as all getout. But you may incur some extra expenses for broken beading needles, you may find it tiring and frustrating to keep fighting the leather to push the needle through, and when you get done, you will have a beautiful piece of beadwork on a very stiff, heavy base. Moccasins, anybody?

By far the easiest surface to work bead embroidery on, and the one I use for trying out new stitches and colorways, is a piece of solid color cotton fabric bonded to a piece of felt. I always bring a stack of these sample blanks to bead embroidery classes, but you can make your own quite easily; all you need is a solid cotton fabric, Wonder Under, and felt. Wonder Under is a paper-backed fusible webbing; you'll find it in the fabric store wherever they keep the bolts of interfacing, usually at one end of the cutting table. Any smooth felt will do; the cheap stuff you find at a crafts store, already cut into 8 ½ x 11 sheets, works just fine. I don't recommend you use the sticky-backed felt sheets for this, however; my needle gets all gunked up going through whatever they use to make them sticky.

To make a sample blank, cut your felt to a convenient size for handwork. Cut out Wonder Under and cotton fabric the same size. Lay the Wonder Under on the felt, sticky side down and paper side up, and press briefly with a hot iron. Let it cool, then gently peel the paper off. (Be careful to leave the fusible web on the felt when you peel off the paper – sometimes it tries to come with.) Put your fabric square on the fusible web and felt combination, right side up, and press with a hot iron until the web has melted and the fabric is fully adhered to the felt.

Okay. That's the firm yet yielding, smooth, easily marked surface for making samples. Presumably you don't want to spend your whole life making samples; you want something you can use and enjoy. What are some options?

If you're going to cover the entire work surface with beads, you can work on Ultrasuede scraps, stiff interfacing, or Lacey's Stiff Stuff. (See list of suppliers in back). If you're not going to cover the entire surface (and many embroidery stitches are open work, which means your work surface will show through) then the same materials are good, but you might want to decorate them a little. Ultrasuede coated with Jones Tones metallic foils gives you a brilliant gold or colored metallic surface to work on. Interfacing and Lacey's Stiff Stuff can be painted with acrylic paints; they dry quickly and you can use the paint to block out broad areas of your design.

If you want to get fancier, try using Wonder Under to bond scraps of lame', satin, silk, lace, etc. to a stabilizing base such as Ultrasuede, felt, or interfacing. You might want to add a very sheer top layer of tulle or fine chiffon to make sure the edges of the scraps don't come up and fray while you're sewing.

Some (but not all!) bead embroidery stitches work well to decorate a simple stuffed doll form. If that's what you're working with, I'd suggest you try out the stitches on a flat sample blank first, then decide whether they'll give the effect you want on a 3D shape.

And, of course, if you're embellishing a crazy quilt block, then you just work directly over the seams of that block.

There's a lot more you can do to create an interesting fabric base for bead embroidery – so much that it deserves a book, or at least a chapter, of its own. For inspiration and suggestions, take a look at Jan Beaney's <u>Stitch Magic</u>, Gwen Hedley's <u>Surfaces for Stitch</u>, Maggie Grey's <u>Raising the Surface</u>, or Valerie Campbell-Harding's <u>Fabric Painting for Embroidery</u>. These books are intended for people doing traditional thread embroidery by hand or machine, but there's no reason we can't adapt the ideas to bead embroidery. Many of the innovative techniques described create a stiff, layered surface, which is wonderful – you don't have to worry about bonding felt or interfacing to stabilize something that's already 4 layers thick and stiff enough to stand up on its own.

Embroidery for Beaders

If you're familiar with beadwork but haven't done much hand embroidery, a good basic stitch dictionary might be a useful adjunct to this book. (See Bibliography in back of book.)

Sharon Boggon's Collection of Stitches (http://inaminuteago.com/stitchindex.html#contents) is a very useful online guide to embroidery stitches.

The question beaders most frequently ask me, when working on these stitches, is "When you say bring the needle up at A, string on so many beads, and bring it down at B, *how far apart* should A and B be?" I've tried to give estimated distances whenever possible, but these are *estimates*, not cast-in-concrete measurements.

When somebody asked Lincoln how long a man's legs should be, he answered, "Long enough to reach the ground."

When you ask me how far apart A and B should be, the only true answer is, "Far enough to create the effect you want." A little common sense and a look at the diagrams will usually tell you more than any arbitrary measurement. If you've strung on 8 seed beads and you want a straight line of 8 seed beads on your fabric, like this:

then obviously A and B should be exactly 8 seed bead lengths apart – and how far that is in fractions of an inch depends on the seed beads *you* are using. You don't want the stitch to look like this

or this

and so you adjust your stitch length to fit your beads.

If you look at one of the books I've recommended, you'll see a lot of stitches that depend on looping threads around each other, or using one stitch to pull the thread of the previous stitch into place, and you may wonder, "How the heck do they do that with beads?"

Chain stitch

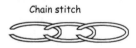

Feather stitch

There are different solutions to this problem. For some stitches I haven't come up with a solution (maybe you will!) but all the stitches discussed in this book can be done in beadwork – including the ones shown at left. I'll discuss various solutions in the next chapter.

Beadwork for embroiderers

If you're familiar with basic embroidery stitches but haven't done much beadwork before, you need to know a little something about the tools and materials beaders use.

Needles

For starters, put away all your embroidery needles with their nice big eyes. They won't go through the beads we're going to use.

If you have quilting needles, also called "betweens", in size 10 or smaller (remember that the eye size gets smaller as the number goes up, so 11's are smaller than 10's are smaller than 9's) those will probably work in the sense that they'll go through the beads. I don't like to do bead embroidery with quilting needles because they're so short; I feel as if I don't have anything to hold on to. However, some people are quite comfortable with them.

Beading needles are long, flexible and have **very** small eyes, the better to go through your beads with. You can usually find beading needles in size 10 or 12 at a general-purpose craft store like Michael's or Hobby Lobby; for smaller sizes you may have to go to a bead shop or order from one of the on-line sources listed in the appendix. Since my eyes are getting older and threading the needle is becoming challenging, I usually work with a size 10 beading needle and change to a smaller size only when I really have to.

Thread

Any time you get three beaders together, you'll get three passionate and different opinions on the best beading thread to use. In my experience, the most commonly used are Nymo and Silamide, with a newcomer, C-lon, gaining ground.

Silamide is a pre-waxed nylon thread, very strong, and has been my personal preference for many years. It comes in a limited range of colors, but the range has been expanding recently; there are more than 20 colors available. If you're offered a choice of sizes, what you want is size "A".

Some people find Silamide hard to thread because it is a "plied" thread (two or more filaments twisted together) but I find it easy to thread; just snip your thread end off at an angle, using sharp scissors, and if the filaments try to separate, drag the thread end through some beeswax to remind it who's boss. The major downsides of Silamide for a new beader are that it's not easy to find in stores, so you have to order it, and it's hard to find small quantities online; I've seen it sold at bead shows on cards, but most of the online suppliers I'm familiar with carry it in 900 or 1000-yard spools, which will cost you around $5.00 apiece. You can get 100-yard spools at www.7echoes.com for $3.50 each, but it's still pricey to build up a collection of different colors.

Nymo is the thread preferred by a majority of beaders, so you have a good chance of finding it at your local bead store or even at Hobby Lobby. It comes in about 30 colors and you can buy it in bobbins holding about 60 yards for under $1.00 a bobbin, so you can acquire a good color selection without breaking the bank (although you may have to order online; I don't think many stores carry anything but white and black). You probably want size "D", although if you decide to work with antique seed beads, which are smaller than most modern ones, you may have to go to size "B" or "0" or "00." (Hey, don't blame me. *I* didn't invent the nomenclature.)

I can't tell you much about Nymo because I don't use it; it doesn't like me. It shreds, it breaks, it refuses to go through the needle, it snarls. You want to use Nymo, go talk to some beaders who like the stuff; there are plenty of them around.

C-lon beading thread has just come on the market recently. It's a nylon monofilament thread that comes in 36 colors, and you can buy it in small bobbins. It seems to stretch less than either Nymo or Silamide, I find it easy to thread and work with, and it's very strong. The only problem I've had with it is when going back through the same bead 3 or 4 times; it seems to be less cooperative than Silamide about scrunching down to let another thread through, probably because it doesn't stretch as much. It will probably become my bead embroidering thread of choice because of the strength, ease of threading, and wide color range. Foxden Designs (see Suppliers) carries C-lon on bobbins.

Beads and sequins

Okay, this is the fun part, right? *Finally* we get to talk about all those lovely, sparkly, shiny, glitzy objects of desire.

In general I have a highly unstructured approach to supplies: if it has a hole through it and isn't too hot or too heavy I will try to bead with it. If it doesn't have a hole through it I will bead around it, and if it's too big for that I will bead over it (assuming it stands still long enough).

However, there are lots of beads (and other objects) that I wouldn't use for bead embroidery on fabric. Those beautiful, big round glass-over-foil beads your aunt brought back from Venice? Save them to make a necklace with; they're not good for bead embroidery. If you try to stitch one directly to the fabric your thread will have to reaaaaaaaaaaaach up to the center hole, leaving long stretches of it exposed:

The perils of embroidering with really big beads

 If you try to use it in a dangle, it'll weigh down the rest of your beads, probably stretch the thread, and possibly injure you if you turn around too quickly while wearing your beadwork.

For most bead embroidery I try not to use round beads more than 4mm in diameter. Long skinny beads are ok. Flat beads are ok. Big fat beads are just more trouble than they're worth.

For the purposes of this volume the bead selection is even more restricted, because for the rest of the book I'm going to be talking about ways to adapt traditional embroidery stitches to beadwork. A lot of this involves taking a string of beads and pretending it's a big thick embroidery thread. Now what kind of beads are best at pretending to be a thick but smooth embroidery thread? Right! Seed beads!

Ninety percent of the work we're going to discuss is going to be done with seed beads and their cousins, bugle beads. So you need to have some idea of what the numbers on those packets of seed and bugle beads mean, what the descriptions mean, and where to get the good stuff, before you go off to build your bead stash.

Seed beads are usually under 2mm in diameter, which is what makes them ideal for this kind of bead embroidery. Their size is indicated by a number like 6/0, 11/0, or 13/0. What are the slash and the 0 for? I have no idea. When someone talks about size 11 seed beads, they mean the beads that are designated 11/0 in a catalog; that's one thing you need to know about the numbering system. The other thing you need to know is: the *higher* the number, the *smaller* the bead. Logical? Oh, don't worry your pretty little head about *logic*. Next thing we know, you'll be trying to correlate those bead numbers with something in the real world, like the number of beads to the inch or the size of needle you need, neither of which works reliably. The best we can do here is comparisons. If the beads you are working with are too big and clunky, find a bigger number (and smaller beads); if they're too small to see without an electron microscope, look for a smaller number (and bigger beads).

Matching needle sizes to bead sizes: If you fall in love with some 15/0 beads (translation: really small) and discover that the needle you're working with is too big to fit through your beads, look for a needle with a higher number (and smaller eye). If you can't see to thread the new needle, maybe you should give up your love affair with the 15/0 beads and look for some bigger ones.

Reasoning like this has led me to a deep and abiding affection for size 11/0 beads, which can usually be strung using a size 10 needle (I told you not to try for exact correlations) which *has an eye big enough for me to see.* For this extremely logical and scientific reason, size 11 beads are the standard used in this book. If I forget to specify the size of beads to use in a given stitch, just assume they should be 11's.

One other note about seed bead sizing numbers: Size 6/0 beads are also called E beads, and that's how I usually refer to them. Habit, that's all. I have no earthly idea <u>why</u> they're called E beads.

Bugle beads are made from long skinny tubes, chopped into somewhat longer segments, Usually they are not not tumbled and reheated to round the ends, which means they may have sharp edges which can cut your thread; for this reason I usually recommend buffering bugle beads with a seed bead at each end of the stitch. The size numbering system for bugles is even more quirky than that for seed beads and what's more, *the numbers run the opposite direction from seed beads*: the larger the number, the longer the bead.. This would, of course, seem perfectly logical if you hadn't just got used to the opposite system prevailing with seed beads and needles. Most bugle beads are about the same diameter as a #11 seed bead, so you principally have to worry about length. A #1 bugle bead will be very very short – hard to tell from a seed bead, even. A #2 bugle bead will probably be 4 to 4.5 mm long, but I've seen companies that define "#2" as 3 mm and others that define it as 6 mm. From there they go on up to bugles as long as 35 mm. Except in fringes and dangles, the very long bugle beads aren't too practical for bead embroidery stitches; they force you to make great big stitches and you really don't want to put them on anything that's going to bend, because they <u>will</u> break, trust me. When I say to use bugle beads for the stitches in this book, unless I say otherwise, I mean your average 4 to 4.5mm bugle bead. The exact length doesn't really matter too much, as long as all the bugle beads you use in a particular stitch are the same length; if you're combining 4 mm beads from one manufacturer with 4.5mm beads from another manufacturer, the stitch isn't going to work out the way it looks in the diagrams and pictures.

Types of seed and bugle beads

Your average shaped, roundish, smooth edged, plain vanilla seed beads are also called <u>rocailles</u>. Seed beads are made by drawing out very long thin tubes and chopping them into itty bitty segments. For rocailles, the segments are then rotated at high heat until their edges get smooth and draw in slightly, like this:

Rocaille

This shape makes them an ideal beginner's bead, because it's easy to find the rounded, slightly sunken edges around the hole with the tip of your needle, the smooth edges won't cut your thread; and they are available in lots of colors, sizes and finishes. So if you're just putting together your bead stash, you might want to start with rocailles – but don't necessarily stop there, because the great variety in styles of seed beads leads to variety in texture, and this is a Good Thing when you're trying to design interesting bead embroideries.

Two-cuts or hex cuts are seed-bead-length segments cut from hexagonal tubes.

Three-cuts are two-cuts with the ends faceted by grinding – very sparkly.

(Just to make your life interesting, it's hard to find 2-cuts and 3-cuts in size 11/0; in fact, I don't know of any sources. 9/0 and 12/0 are the usual sizes. There appears to be a streak of anarchy in the bead manufacturing world. Or maybe it's sadism.)

Charlottes are seed beads with one facet ground flat, which gives them a lovely bright and sparkly appearance. For some reason known only to bead manufacturers, charlottes are usually size 13. (If they came in 11's, I'd use a lot more of them.)

Maccas, also known as hex bugles and cut bugles, are bugle beads with hexagonal cross sections.

Twisted bugle beads are just what you'd expect them to be: they look as if somebody took a tube that wasn't quite round in cross section and twisted it like a candy cane. They're pretty and glittery and hard to find.

Delicas are the aristocracy of seed beads. Somewhat smaller in outside diameter than 11's, they are cylindrical rather than rounded. (. "Delica" is a trade mark of Miyuki Shoji Corp. Toho Corp. manufactures similar beads named "Antiques")

Delica

People who do bead loom work, where having beads of uniform size is crucial, love Delicas and will tell you without qualification that they are the BEST seed beads available and that you should never buy anything else.

Ahem.

For what we're going to be doing, absolute uniformity of beads is not required; in fact, it can be rather boring. And Delicas are considerably more expensive than most other seed beads.

That being said, I will admit to having a non-trivial stash of Delicas, because they do have advantages other than uniformity. They come in a very wide range of colors; they're handy to use when you need to squeeze some beads into a tight corner that isn't quite big enough for the 11's you've been using; and best of all, they have holes you can drive a truck through, which is *really* good for some stitches where you have to pass the thread through the same bead three or four times.

Finishes for seed and bugle beads

If you don't see anything about the finish of a bead, it's probably a glossy transparent or opaque bead.

Brightly colored opaque seed beads are used in many ethnic bead embroideries, such as Native American beadwork, Zulu beadwork, etc. They're good for showing off detailed patterns but they don't work well with most other seed bead finishes.

Transparent seed beads with no decorative finish or lining are hard to find, probably because they allow the background material to show through and most people don't care for that effect. However, they can have a special glow when worked over material that has been painted or treated with a metallic foil; I collect transparent beads for just that reason.

Aurora Borealis (AB)or rainbow beads have a rainbow-like coating through which the original bead color shines through.

An iris finish is heavier and more metallic than AB.

Scarabee is a very heavy iris finish, usually applied over black glass to produce a dark finish with green, purple or blue highlights.

<u>Galvanized</u> beads have been even more heavily coated with metal particles, to the point where the original color of the bead is completely covered. Most are very bright, real eye-catchers. Some beaders have trouble with galvanized finishes wearing off as they work with them; this hasn't been a problem for me, so it probably has something to do with the exact chemical content of your sweat. The only way you can find out for sure is to try working with some. Another potential problem with galvanized beads is that the coating can rub off if you apply the beads to something that will suffer friction or abrasion. (In other words, don't throw your beadwork in the washer. But you weren't going to do that anyway, were you?)

<u>Matte</u> finish seed beads have a non-reflective, slightly roughened surface. Think super-fine-grit sandpaper here, not craters of the moon. They'll look smooth to the naked eye but you will be able to feel the difference between these and glossy beads. Some may have started life as transparents, but after the shiny finish has been removed (usually with an acid bath) they will be translucent at best. If they started out opaque, of course, they'll still be opaque. Matte finishes provide an interesting texture contrast to the shiny finishes common on most beads. Incidentally, you can "matte" your own beads by dipping them in a product called Dip 'n Etch.

<u>Matte AB</u> or <u>ghost</u> beads have a matte finish with soft iridescent highlights.

<u>Alabaster</u> or <u>opal</u> beads are made from glass filled with tiny crystalline particles that make it look opaque or semi-opaque without the hard bright finish characteristic of beads described simply as "opaque."

<u>Satin</u> beads have a smooth finish, less brilliant than glossy beads but shinier than matte ones.

<u>Luster</u> beads have, well, a lustrous surface – sort of like pearls.

<u>Ceylon</u> or <u>Ceylon pearl</u> beads are lustered beads that began life as alabaster beads.

<u>Silver-lined</u> transparent beads have a metallic silver coating inside the hole that makes them very bright, as the light bounces off the silver and passes back through the colored glass.Until recently I had not seen any metallic lined beads except in silver, but now it's possible to find <u>copper-lined</u> transparent beads also. The copper color can give added warmth to transparent beads on the warm side of the color wheel (yellow, pink, red, magenta, reddish purple) but may dull cool colors like blue or green; I can't really describe the effect of a copper lining on blue or green glass except to say that it's, well, interesting, and you should try to look at some before you buy.

<u>Color-lined</u> transparent beads have a color dyed or painted inside the hole which either enhances or dulls down the color of the glass. This color may not hold up to energetic stringing in which you slide the bead around on the thread or shove the

thread through it three or four times; experiment before using color-lined beads in a major project.

Dyed beads are just that – dyed – and the color may come off with handling or washing. It's probably a good idea to test any dyed beads you plan to use by leaving a few in a dish of bleach, alcohol, or nail polish remover for a few minutes, to see how much color can come off. You may wonder why anybody would bother with these beads when there are so many other colors and finishes available; well, some colors are very hard to get in glass without resort to dyeing – true, strong purples and vibrant pinks come to mind. (I happen to like true, strong purples and vibrant pinks.)

Believe it or not, there are actually more finishes and treatments, but most of them are variations on these variations. Anyway, I'm tired of finish names, and I expect you are too. The list above will give you a good start at deciphering the descriptions in bead catalogs, but ultimately there's no sure thing except actually looking at the beads.

Other stuff

To make the most of the embroidery-type stitches described in the following chapters, you will want a few beads other than seeds and bugles. Smallish decorative beads are good for adding accents to the end or beginning of a stitch, raising the middle of a line of beads, adding texture, and so forth. Any or all of the following will serve you well: 6/0 or E beads, gemstone chips, shell heishi, small Swarovski crystals (remember the 4mm rule!), small fire polished crystals (less expensive than Swarovskis, but also less brilliant), the cube and triangle beads made by Miyuki, small drop beads (tear-drop shaped, with a hole through the narrow part), small freshwater pearls.

Sequins are also good for adding interest, not to mention glitz, to bead embroidery. Round ones are easiest to use because no matter how they spin round on the thread, they'll look the same in the stitch; square ones are a little trickier but worth the trouble for the contrast they give; stars and other novelty shapes can turn a simple bead embroidery stitch into a wild fantasy stitch; holographic sequins are unparalleled for glitz but may overpower your beadwork.

Where beads come from, what to look for, and where to get them

Nearly all seed beads are made in the Czech Republic or in Japan. Japanese seed beads are somewhat more expensive and tend to be more regular in shape and hole size than the Czech beads; this isn't such a big deal for bead embroidery as it is for some other types of bead work, but if you have low tolerance for discovering that your needle won't go through the bead you just picked up, you might be happier with the Japanese-made beads. On the other hand, Czech beads are usually sold in hanks (12-20 loops of prestrung beads tied together at the top) and Japanese beads are usually sold in bags. Those prestrung beads really speed up the work when you're doing something like a BCB chain stitch that calls for 14-18 beads on the needle with each stitch; you just line the thread of the hank up with your needle and slip all 14-18 beads on with one motion. So it's your call. Me, I have Czech beads and Japanese beads and Taiwanese beads; I have beads in sizes from 6 to 14; my philosophy is, if the bead exists and you like the look of it, buy it. In fact, buy a whole hank of it if you can.

You may want to start off a little slower than that.

Any large crafts store will have a bead section and will sell you little packets of seed beads, and this is a quick and easy way to get started; just pick up five or six packages of beads in colors you like or at least can put up with. You'll pay as much for a handful of beads as you would for a whole hank from a bead supplier, the color choice will be abysmal and the quality will not be much better, and they'll probably be a nominal size 9/0 which is really too big for most embroidery stitches. But you'll have the beads, and it's instant gratification...of a sort. And you just may get lucky; the Hobby Lobby nearest my house has started carrying a decent selection of Delicas. I hope this is a trend.

Take a small step upward and look in the needlework section of the crafts store, or of a good needlework store if you have one nearby, and you'll find Mill Hill beads, which are somewhat better quality. They will come in <u>really</u> small plastic boxes, they'll cost even more per bead than the junky packages did, but the color selection and quality will be better and you'll be able to find smaller beads.

If there is a bead shop in your town, that will be your best starting place. Here you can hope to find a reasonably good selection of both Czech and Japanese seed beads and Delicas, needles and beading thread, and – with luck – knowledgeable salespeople who love their work and will be happy to advise you. A word of warning, though: most of the bead shops I've visited have been oriented more towards stringing large beads than towards seed bead work or embroidery. Try not to go overboard on big beautiful beads, ok? Flat ones will work with some bead embroidery techniques but not with most of the stuff in this book. Big heavy round beads really aren't suited to bead embroidery, and ...ok, ok, I see you fingering those 12mm ocean jasper spheres...put them down! Now! And get back over to the seed bead section where you belong.

Check local bead and ornament societies and find out if they have a yearly show and if so, when it is. This will be your chance to run your fingers through hanks of seed and bugle beads in all colors of the rainbow and to talk to some people who actually know and care about their merchandise. Check out gem and mineral shows, too; there are usually a lot of vendors selling materials that you can use in embroidery, such as strings of gemstone chips, freshwater pearls, and cabochons in all the colors of the rainbow.

And finally, when you're seriously addicted, try shopping online at some of the sites listed in the back of the book. The big suppliers have an unparalleled selection of beads in all sizes, colors and finishes, and in no time at all you can build a bead stash that will supply your every need...well, almost. There'll always be that elusive color, or that string of perfect pearls you bought in '02 and have never seen anywhere since, or the design that requires you to shop all over the Internet for 6 different values of green lustered seed beads.

CHAPTER TWO: CONVERTING EMBROIDERY TO BEADWORK

Simple stitches

Some embroidery stitches have a fairly straightforward translation into beadwork. I call these *simple* stitches. You bring the needle up through the fabric, you string on a certan number of beads, you bring the needle down and you're done. Your next stitch may need to be placed in a specific position relative to the first stitch, but you're never going to go back to those first beads and move or interfere with them in any way.

Examples of simple stitches are satin stitch

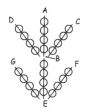

and fern stitch.

Compound stitches

However, many embroidery stitches are based on the expectation that you'll make a loop of some sort with your first stitch that will be held in place by the next stitch. I call these **compound** stitches. Examples of compound stitches are fly stitch

and chain stitch.

In order to work with compound stitches, or even to use some of the more interesting variations of the simple stitches, you need to make a decision about how you're going to handle the places where, in ordinary embroidery, one thread would cross another and hold it in place.

With conventional embroidery there's only one way to do this; with bead embroidery you have a choice of three techniques (maybe more; I've only been able to think of three, but there may be some more out there.)

I call these three techniques BCB (Beads Crossing Beads), TCT (Thread Crossing Thread), and SBT (Stitch Back Through a bead). It's worth while becoming familiar with them, because they have very different looks, and because not all stitches and variations can be worked with just one technique: you need all three to make the most of your bead embroidery.

In discussing particular compound stitches I'll give step-by-step directions on how to use each technique (when applicable) and will also discuss what results you can expect and why I sometimes favor one technique for a given stitch even if two, or all three, are technically applicable. However, it might be useful to familiarize yourself with the techniques themselves before worrying about how they're used in particular stitches. That's what this section is for. If you're fairly comfortable with bead embroidery and don't want to waste time on preliminaries, skip this and go directly to the stitches; if you aren't quite sure how these three techniques work, you might want to try out the following directions on a nice, firm, smooth fabric surface before going on to look at different stitches.

Beads crossing beads (BCB):

First pass: bring the needle up at A, string 8-10 seed beads, and take the needle down again at B, about ¼" away.

Be sure to draw the first loop of beads tight against the cloth so that no thread is showing between the beads.

Second pass: bring up the needle at C, inside the first loop, near the point where you want this loop held down, and string on the second set of beads. Draw these down tight against the cloth, so that no thread shows between the beads.

Hold these beads in place with your free thumb and forefinger while you insert your needle on the outside of the first loop, at D, and bring the thread taut against the cloth.

Thread crossing thread (TCT):

Bring the needle up at A, string 12 seed beads, and take the needle down again at B, about ¼" away.. Leave a little slack in the loop so that you can see thread between the two beads where you will stitch down in a moment. (Many stitches are symmetrical and will work best if you string on an even number of seed beads for this loop, so that you have the same number of beads on each side of the crossing you are about to create.)

Second pass: bring the needle up at C on the inside of the loop, right against the thread. Pull the thread taut so that it crosses the thread of the first pass right between two beads.

For some stitches you'll then bring the needle down right away without putting on any beads in the second pass, so that you're just catching the thread of the first pass with a tiny stitch. To do this just bring the needle down at D, immediately on the other side of the loop.

Most stitches require you to thread on some beads for the second pass, which requires a little more coordination. Let's say we want an anchor stitch of three seed beads; you come up at C, bring the thread across and hold it there with your thumb, string 3 seed beads, and bring the needle down at D, a little farther away from the loop than in the previous picture.

Stitching back through a bead (SBT):

Bring needle up at A, string on nine seed beads, and come down at B, about ¼" away.

(For symmetrical stitches, you want to start with an odd number of beads, so that the bead you stitch back through is located in the exact center of the loop.

Flatten this loop of beads against the cloth and notice where the center bead lies. Now bring the needle up at C, outside the loop and just beside the center bead.

Stitch through the center bead and bring the needle down at D, just on the other side of the bead, pinning the loop down there.

[Tip: If you are having a hard time recognizing which is the center bead, try using a contrasting color; for instance, you might start by stringing on 4 white, 1 gray, and 4 white beads.

Then you'll be able to tell at a glance where your stitching-down thread should go.]

Notation

There isn't much of it. You'll see the three abbreviations BCB, TCT, and SBT so many times that you won't have any trouble remembering what they stand for. The only other bit of notation that might be confusing is the description of stringing sequences. Many bead embroidery stitches call for stringing ten to twenty beads at one time, often in some specific sequence of colors and/or styles. Instead of spelling out stringing sequences word for word, I use the abbreviations seq (sequin), Eb (6/0 or E bead), bb (bugle bead) and sb (come on, you can guess what that stands for, can't you?) And I put the abbreviations in parentheses so that you can recognize a stringing sequence at a glance.

In other words: instead of saying, "String three seed beads, one bugle bead, one seed bead, one E bead, one seed bead, one bugle bead, and three seed beads" I'll say "String the sequence (3sb, bb, sb, Eb, sb, bb, 3sb). There! That wasn't so painful, was it?

CHAPTER THREE: BACK STITCH

Basic Back Stitch

This is for sewing one line of beads at a time onto fabric, and a very good stitch it is, too. Unfortunately, it's about all you see in many bead embroideries. It is an extremely versatile and useful stitch, and it's a good starting place....but I hope you won't stop there!

Note: For most stitches I will show the view from above, as if you were looking down on the beaded fabric. For this stitch, though, we all know what the view from above looks like: a line of beads! I'm going to show a side view, as if you cut the fabric right alongside your sewing line and held it up and squinted at it, ok?

Bring needle up at A, string on 4 beads, down at B.

Come back up at C, pass needle back beads 3 and 4, string on 4-5 more beads,  through down at D.

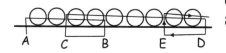 Come back up at E, string back through beads 7 and 8, string on 4-5 more beads, and so on.

It's the fact of the needle passing through the previous beads of each stitch that makes this look like a nice, smooth, unbroken line of beads even though it is created with many short little stitches.

The exact number of beads, of course, depends on circumstances. When working a tight curve, I may get down to where I'm adding on only 2 beads with each stitch. When working a long straight line of Delicas or other small beads, I'll probably put them on 6 at a time.

Extremely Secure Basic Back Stitch

When I'm doing work that's going to be handled a lot or put in the washer, or when I'm using the back stitch as a launching pad for various raised or fringing techniques, or even when I'm working around a line with very tight curves, I tend to go from the basic back stitch to an even more repetitive (and more secure) stitch.

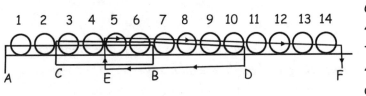

Begin by bringing the needle up at A, stringing on 6 seed beads, and bringing the needle down at B.

Bring the needle up again at C, between beads 2 and 3. Pass needle back through beads 3-6, string on 4 new beads, and stitch down at D.

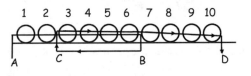

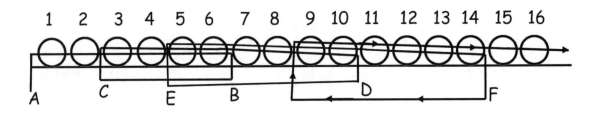

Come up at E, between beads 4 and 5. Pass needle back through beads 5-10, string on 4 new beads and stitch down at F.

Continue in this way, going back through 6 beads and adding 4 each time.

Notice that the string of beads is anchored to the cloth every 2 beads, and except for the first two beads, every bead is held down by at least 2 passes of the thread. (I usually start this way because I'm usually working in a circle or some approximation thereof, so I'll go back through those last 2 beads when I close the circle. If you're doing a line that doesn't close back on itself, start with 4 beads instead of 6.)

Repeating Back Stitch

If you want to work a linear pattern – say, repeated lines of stitching bordering a shape, like echo quilting - it's easy to do with back stitch. As long as all your beads are the same size, you are essentially drawing a line one bead thick on the fabric, and you can go back and draw a second line right next to it and keep going that way indefinitely.

In the first example of repeating back stitch on the color pictures page, four colors of seed beads are used to create an undulating line. By starting each new line of back stitch slightly below the preceding one, you get a look of beads sort of dripping over a gentle series of edges.

Of course, there's no law that you have to stitch with just one type or size or color of bead! It's possible to work a very close series of lines using beads of different sizes, if you're careful. Two lines of size 11 seed beads will fill about the same space as a size 6 (E) bead, so you can work your first line of backstitch alternating sequences of seed beads with E beads. Then work the second line using seed beads only, passing through the E beads of the first line whenever you come to them.

In the pictured example I worked four lines of back stitch in this style, following a gently curving line. If you look closely, you'll see that some fudging is necessary to follow the curves; inner curves require one seed bead between E beads instead of two, outer curves require three, and after that comes a point where you may need to add or delete E beads in subsequent lines.

Whipped Back Stitch

After completing a line of back stitch, go back and take short stitches over and across the line, using beads of a contrasting color or texture.

Threaded Back Stitch

After completing a line of back stitch, go back to the beginning. Bring the needle up at A, thread 3 to 5 seed beads in a contrasting color and bring the needle under the line of back stitch. Take a very small stitch through the fabric at B, right under the back stitched beads and coming up on the other side at B1.

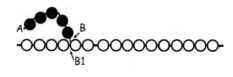

Repeat on this side and continue in this fashion to the end of the original line. This can be worked tight and close to the original line of stitching or it can be used to make gentle curves on either side of the line.

[Note: In traditional thread embroidery this stitch is worked without the interlacing thread passing through the fabric at all, and can be made into a very tight ornamented stitch. With beadwork I find it better to take a small stitch through the material instead of literally weaving under the line of beads. You're not going to pull a string of beads through such a small space anyway;the stitch gives you a chance to anchor the string of beads and, if you're having tension problems, to take a small back stitch for additional security.]

Double Threaded Back Stitch

Work a single threaded back stitch and when you are done, go back and work loops threaded on the opposite sides. You don't have to use the same kind of beads – you can use one kind for the first threading and another for the second threading, as  shown in this diagram. Or you can use a different type or color of seed bead for each loop, or a set of different beads within each loop – which is way too complicated to diagram!

Drop Beads Back Stitch

Drop seed beads or Magatamas, with their off-center holes, make a simple backstitch look like some kind of fancy braiding. They naturally flip so as to line up on alternate sides of the thread.

Pekinese Stitch

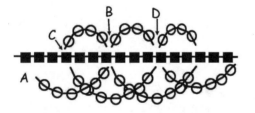

Work a line of simple back stitch; then take a contrasting color of beads and work back through the line as follows: Bring needle on at A and string on enough beads to make a gentle loop before coming down at B. Take a tiny stitch through the material and come up just the other side of the line of back stitched beads, so that it looks as if you were weaving the new beads under the first line. String on 3 or 4 beads – about half as many as you had between A and B – and bring needle down at C, repeating the tiny stitch under the line and coming up on the side where you started. String on 7-8 beads, as many as you used from A to B. Pass the needle under the A-B loop and bring it down at D. Continue as shown in diagram.

Half Pekinese Stitch

I really don't know what to call this stitch; it's one I worked out for myself after deciding that I liked the side of the Pekinese stitch with the overlapping lines better than the side with the short loops. So you basically take that half of the Pekinese stitch and work it on either side of the line of back stitch, as follows:

Bring needle up at A, string on 6-8 seed beads for a graceful loop (remember, it must have some slack in it, because you're going to pass another loop under it in a minute!) and bring needle down at B. Bring needle up again at C, string on 6-8 seed beads and bring down at D. Come up at E, string on 6-8 seed beads, pass the line under the loop A-B and come down at F. Come up again at G and continue in this fashion, working side to side alternately.

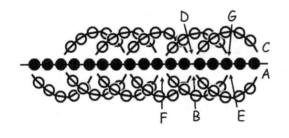

If you prefer, there's no reason why you can't work all of one side first and then all of the other. Or use one color of seed beads on one side and one color on another. Or change seed bead colors as you go along.
Half Pekinese stitch can be very useful for making a smooth gradation between a central line of relatively large backstitched beads and a border of smaller beads; take a look at the example on the color pictures page.

Overlapping Back Stitch

Short lines of back stitch worked in overlapping fashion can create a broad, undulating line. A similar effect can be obtained with satin stitch, but back stitch allows you to make the individual lines longer and to introduce a curve in the lines if you wish.

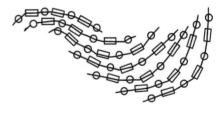

Back Stitch with Dangles

It's easy to add a dangle after every few beads of back stitch, but it does require an extra pass through some beads, so you want to pick seed beads with relatively large holes.

Let's say you want to put a dangle after every four beads. Begin as for basic back stitch: needle up at A, string on four beads, needle down at B. Bring needle back up at C and pass through the last two beads of the previous stitch.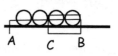

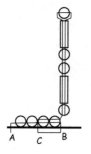

Now, instead of continuing with the basic back stitch, insert your dangle sequence. Here I'm using a fairly short and simple sequence of (sb, bb, 2sb, bb, sb). String this on, use the last seed bead as a pivot and go back through the remaining beads of the dangle.

Now go down at B, up at C, go through the last two beads of the first stitch again and you're ready to start your next back stitch.

The diagram above shows how the thread passes through the bead and the fabric but isn't a very realistic depiction of what the completed stitch looks like. When you've done a series of this you'll have a sort of sparse fringe like the diagram to the right.

Worked in isolation on a plain background, as in the color picture, this isn't very interesting. However, it can be a way to add texture and interest to a series of rows of plain back stitch. In the projects section (Chapter 18) you'll see how it can be used to frame the face and build "hair" for a beaded doll or a figural pin.

CHAPTER FOUR: BUTTONHOLE STITCH

Basic Buttonhole Stitch

This is a compound stitch, which means you're going to have to choose a crossing technique when working it. Any of the three crossing techniques described in Chapter Two will work with the basic buttonhole stitch, though some variations work better with one technique than another. It's also an extremely versatile stitch that you can take far from its beginnings with the humble buttonhole.

Thread Crossing Thread

 Bring needle up at A, string 8 seed beads, bring needle down at B. Hold the loop in place with your thumb so that it forms a right angle between beads 4 and 5, with a little bit of thread showing at that point.

 Bring needle up at C, <u>inside</u> the loop. Draw the thread tight between the 4th and 5th beads of the loop and string on 8 more seed beads.

From here you repeat the steps for the first loop: bring needle down, hold loop in right-angle position, bring needle up inside loop, cross thread and string beads for next loop.

Continue in this fashion until the line is as long as you want it, then finish the last loop with a simple holding-down stitch over the thread between beads 4 and 5.

Beads Crossing Beads

Bring needle up at A, string on 8 seed beads, and bring needle down at B. You want the loop of 8 seed beads to lie flat on the fabric and form a right angle, just as for TCT, but in this case you don't want any thread showing between the beads.

As usual with the BCB technique, you will need 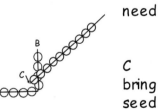 slightly more beads on each loop from here out, because each loop has to pass up and over the beads of the previous loop. So bring the needle up at C and string on 10 seed beads. At this point, before you bring your needle down at D, it's a good idea to draw the seed beads down until they are held closely against the fabric, to make sure that both beads and thread cross over the loop and not just the thread alone.

Bring the string of 10 seed beads down over the loop AB and against the fabric, forming a right angle that ends where you bring the needle down at D.

When you are ready to end the line of stitches, just come up inside the last loop, string on 4 to 6 seed beads, and bring the needle down just outside the loop to anchor it.

In the color pictures I've shown this worked two ways: first with alternating colors, so that you can see the stitch structure better, and then with just one color, so you can see the purely textural effects.

Stitch Back Through

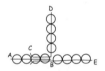 First loop: Bring needle up at A, string 4 beads, down at B.

Come up at C and pass needle through beads 3 and 4 of the previous stitch, then string 4 beads and bring needle down at D.

Second loop: Bring needle up again at C, pass through beads 3 and 4 again, string on 4 more beads and bring needle down at E.

Bring needle up at F, pass through beads 3 and 4 of previous stitch, string 4 beads, bring down at G. Bring needle up at F to begin third loop by passing through beads 11 and 12 again.

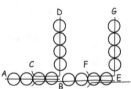

Variable Length Stems

This can be very effective if worked close, with the SBT technique. For the first stitch, thread on just 3 seed beads, come up and go back through the 2nd bead. For the next one, thread on 4 seed beads, come up and go back through the 2nd bead again. Continue to increase the number of beads one at a time until the stitch is as high as you want, then slowly decrease again.

Sequin or Decorative Bead Ends

 This can be done with any of the three crossing methods – TCT, BCB, or SBT. Detailed instructions are given for TCT only.
Bring needle up at A, string (8 sb, seq), bring needle down at B.
Hold the loop in place with your thumb so that
it forms a right angle between beads 4 and 5,
with a little bit of thread showing at that point.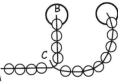
Bring needle up at C, <u>inside</u> the loop. Draw the thread tight
between the 4th and 5th beads of the loop and string on 8
more seed beads and another sequin.

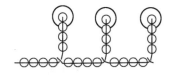 From here you repeat the steps for the first loop: bring needle down, hold loop in right-angle position, bring needle up inside loop, cross thread and string beads for next loop. Continue in this fashion until the line is as long as you want it, then finish the last loop with a simple holding-down stitch over the thread between beads 4 and 5.

If using a larger decorative bead instead of a sequin, you may want to add a seed bead at the end of your sequence to buffer the thread, so that you would string (8 sb, big bead, sb). That's a judgement call – depends how big your decorative bead is and how sharp the edges of the hole are.

Bugle Bead Branches

Thread Crossing Thread

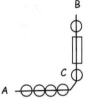

Bring needle up at A. String (5 sb, bb, sb) and bring needle down at B, laying the beads down on the cloth so that they make a more or less right angle at C, between seed beads 4 and 5. (Don't worry if it doesn't look as straight as in the picture. All you really need to do is push the beads into the approximate shape you want so that you know where to cross the thread.)

Bring needle up at C, cross the thread of the previous stitch to hold it in place, and string another (5sb, bb, sb) to form another right angle, which will be held in place when you begin the next stitch.

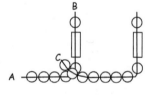

Beads Crossing Beads

Since for BCB each stitch has to go over the "hump" of the previous line of beadwork, after the first stitch you'll need to string 7-8 seed beads at the start of each stitch rather than 5.

First loop: Bring needle up at A, string (5 sb, bb, sb) and bring down at B so that the loop of beads makes a right angle between beads 4 and 5. Draw thread taut so that there are no spaces between the beads.

Second loop: Bring needle up at C, string (8 sb, bb, sb) and bring it down at D. Draw thread taut so that there are no spaces between the beads.

In the color picture illustrating this stitch I was using bugles with nicely rounded edges that didn't need buffering. I worked some of the stitch without a final seed bead and some of it with one, so that you can see both effects.

Stitch Back Through

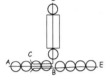
First loop: Bring needle up at A, string 4 beads, down at B. Come up at C and pass needle through beads 3 and 4 of the previous stitch, then string (sb, bb, sb) and bring needle down at D.

Second loop: Bring needle up again at C, pass through beads 3 and 4 again, string on 4 more beads and bring needle down at E.

Bring needle up at F, pass through beads 3 and 4 of previous stitch, string (sb, bb, sb), bring down at G. Bring needle up again at F to begin third loop by passing through beads 11 and 12 again.

Bugle Bead Stem and Branches

This doesn't work so well with the BCB method; I use either SBT or TCT. Described here, and illustrated in the color pictures section, is the TCT method.

Bring needle up at A. String (sb, bb, 2sb, bb. sb) and bring needle down at B, laying the beads down on the cloth so that they make a more or less right angle at C, between the two middle seed beads.

Bring needle up at C, cross the thread of the previous stitch to hold it in place, and string another (sb, bb, 2sb, bb, sb) to form another right angle, which will be held in place when you begin the next stitch.

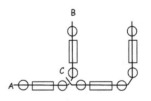

Dangles

This variation is most easily worked with the SBT method. First loop: Bring needle up at A, string 4 seed beads, down at B. Come up at C, pass through beads 3 and 4 of the previous stitch, string (8sb, crystal, sb). Using the last seed bead strung as a pivot bead, pass back through the crystal and the first 8 seed beads and bring needle down at B.

Second loop: Bring needle up at C and pass through beads 3 and 4 again, then string 4 seed beads and bring needle down at D. Come up at E, pass through beads 3 and 4 of the previous stitch, string (8sb, crystal, sb). Using the last seed bead strung as a pivot bead, pass back through the crystal and the first 8 seed beads and bring needle down at D. Come up again at E to begin third loop.

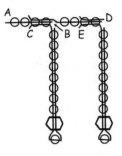

Alternating Stitches

This is an easy variation of the SBT buttonhole stitch: simply work the branches on alternating sides of the main line. Directions and diagram are for a variation with bugle bead branches.

First loop: Bring needle up at A, string 4 seed beads, down at B. Come up at C, stitch back through beads 3 and 4 of the previous stitch, string (sb, bb, sb) and bring needle down at D.

Second loop: Bring needle up at A, string through beads 3 and 4 of the first stitch, string 4 seed beads and bring needle down at E. Come up at F, stitch back through beads 3 and 4 of the previous loop, string (sb, bb, sb) and bring needle down at G, on the opposite side of the line from the first bugle bead branch.

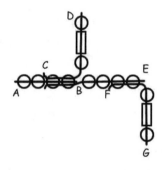

Continue in this manner, bringing the bugle bead stitches down on alternating sides of the base line.

Obviously you can play with all sorts of variations on this theme. The pictured sample shows this stitch worked along an undulating base line. You could also end the

bugle bead stitches with sequins or accent beads, or put dangles along the bottom row, or change colors with each stitch, or combine any number of variations.

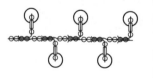

Closed Buttonhole Stitch

I prefer to work this with the TCT method, although it can also be done with BCB for a more textured effect. The bead counts given are for size 11 seed beads and

for a stitch between two parallel lines about ¼ " apart.
First loop: Bring needle up at A, string on 4 seed beads, and down at B

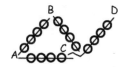

Bring needle up at A again, string on 8 seed beads, and come down at B again, leaving a loose flapping loop which you will tighten with the next loop you make.

Second loop: Come up at C (inside the loop), cross thread over between beads 4 and 5 of the previous stitch, and come down at D.
Come up at C again, cross thread in the same place, string on 8 seed beads and come down at D again.

Third loop: Bring needle up at E, cross threads and continue as for second loop.
[Tip: The bead counts here are made under the assumption that you are making perfect equilateral triangles. If you prefer a pointy triangle or a flattened one, you'll need to adjust the number of beads in each "long" stitch accordingly. Stringing on 7 beads and crossing thread between beads 3 and 4 will slightly exaggerate the top point of the triangle; stringing on 9 beads and crossing between beads 4 and 5 will slightly flatten the triangle. "Slightly" is a key word here! In the pictured sample I was actually trying to make equilateral triangles but wound up having to use 9 beads on each "long" stitch.]

Closed Buttonhole With Bugle Beads (SBT)

This is worked exactly like the regular closed buttonhole stitch, except that instead of stringing seed beads you string sets of (sb, bb, sb).

First loop: Bring needle up at A, string (sb,bb,sb; bring needle down at B. Bring needle up at A again and string (1 sb, 1bb, 2sb, 1 bb, 1 sb) and bring needle down at B again.

Second loop: Bring needle up at C, cross threads between the two seed beads in the middle of the previous stitch, string (1sb, 1bb, 1 sb) and bring needle down at D. Bring needle up at C again and

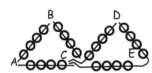

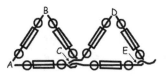

string (1 sb, 1bb, 2sb, 1 bb, 1 sb) and bring needle down at D again.
Third loop: Bring needle up at E, cross threads between the two seed beads in
the middle of the previous stitch, and continue as in second loop.

Closed Buttonhole With Dangles

In the previous two versions of closed buttonhole stitch, we had the triangles
pointing "up," although it really makes no difference which way you work it. For
this version, you definitely want the triangles pointing down.

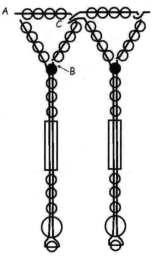

First loop: Bring needle up at A, string on (4sb), then string on
your dangle sequence – here it is (4 sb, bb, 3 sb, Eb, sb). Using
the last seed bead strung as a pivot bead, take the needle back
through the rest of the dangle (the already strung Eb, 3 sb, bb, 4
sb) and now, finally, bring it down at B.
Work the second stitch just like any other
closed buttonhole – needle up at A, string
on 8 sb, down at B.

Second loop: Bring needle up at C, cross
threads of previous stitch between beads
4 and 5, and proceed as for first loop.

*[TIP: When stringing a long sequence of
beads where you'll want to go back
through part but not all of the sequence,
it helps to use a bead of a different color
or texture where the repeat begins. Notice the bead that's
colored black on the diagram? In the pictured example it is
gold in contrast with the pink of the other seed beads –
matches the bugle and E beads I used, and gives me an easy way to see when I've
gone back through all the dangle beads.]*

As with the regular (open) buttonhole stitch, this can be worked in BCB fashion to
give a closer, more textured look.

Circular forms

Buttonhole stitch is great for working circular forms, large or small. A small circle
can be worked with just one stitch, with the same bead count each time.
For a larger circle, assuming you want to fill the space rather than leaving an
open area in the middle, you may want to make only every second stitch long
enough to reach to the center. Not only does this create a pleasing variation, but
it avoids the problem of having all your long stitches crashing together in the
center of the circle where there's not enough room for so many of them.
Working these circular forms is so much fun that you just might decide to pull out
all the stops and make a buttonhole mandala combining a variety of stitch
techniques and beads.

The example on the color pictures page has an outer border of whipped backstitch, but everything else is done with buttonhole stitch.
The "Hands" wall hanging (one of the projects in Chapter 18) uses a large circular form built from successive layers of buttonhole stitch; see that project for a detailed description and diagram.

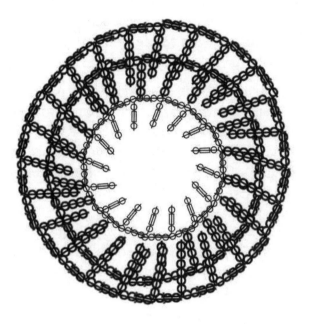

CHAPTER FIVE: CHAIN STITCH

Basic Chain Stitch

This is a compound stitch: you create a series of bead loops, each loop holding down the previous one, and end with a simple stitch to hold the very last loop in place. Any of the three crossing techniques will work here, producing three very different effects. If you're not sure which one you want to use, it might be a good idea to work samples of all three so as to get a feeling for the effect produced.

Bead counts given in the stitch instructions are approximate, as always, intended to give you a starting point rather than an unvarying pattern. You may need to change the number of beads up or down depending on the size of beads you are using, the size of the stitches you make, and the look you want to achieve. When it's important that there be an odd or even number of beads I'll say so in the instructions.

Beads Crossing Beads

To help you keep track of stitches, I'm going to suggest you use two different colors of beads to begin with. This is quite a nifty effect in its own right but right now it has the immeasurable advantage of helping you to be quite clear which loop you're going through at each point.

 Bring the needle up through the fabric at A, string 15-18 white beads (size 11) , and bring it down again at B. You now have a bead loop flopping around on top of your fabric.

Bring the needle up at C and pass your thread through the loop. String 15-18 black beads and bring the needle down at D. If you hold the loop of black beads down with your thumb, you'll see how it holds the loop of white beads in place.

 Of course, now you need another loop to hold this one down. Bring the needle up again at E and pass through the black loop, string 15-17 white beads and bring the needle down at F.

When you get tired of making loops, end the chain by bringing up the thread as at G, stringing on 4-6 beads and bringing the needle down at H.

Thread Crossing Thread

 Bring the needle up at A, string 4 beads and bring it down again at B. (The number of beads may vary, but if you want this stitch to be symmetrical, you must use an *even* number of beads on each loop)

Bring the needle up again at C, pull the thread between beads 2 and 3 of the previous loop, string 4 beads and bring the needle down again at D.

Continue in this fashion;

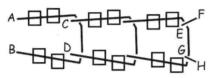 when you are ready to end the chain, take two short finishing stitches across the thread of the last loop as shown at E-F and G-H on the diagram at left.

Stitch Back Through

 Bring the needle up at A, string 9 beads and bring it down again at B. (Just as the TCT method required an even number of beads to make a symmetrical stitch, this requires an odd number of beads.)

Bring the needle up again at C, stitch through the 5th bead on the previous loop, and make another loop of 9 beads.

Continue in this fashion until you are ready to end the chain, then secure the last loop by a short stitch through the middle bead, coming up at D and down at E.

An easy variation on this is to make the center bead larger or of a different color than the other beads in the loop. In the color pictures you will see a version where I used a matte green E bead and strung (4sb, Eb, 4sb).

Filled Chain Stitch

This really has to be worked with the SBT technique, as you need a slightly rounded loop and you need the space within to be open. Stringing an odd number of beads for each stitch, work a series of nicely rounded chain stitches. Your finished stitch should look something like this:

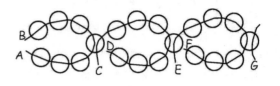

Now go back through and stitch a decorative bead in the center of each loop.

[Tip: The intelligent way to do this is to pick your decorative beads first, then work a sample with the seed beads you want to use to make sure that you have the right number of beads in each chain stitch to frame the decorative bead perfectly. Alternatively, you can do it the way I did the sample, making the line of chain stitches first and then fumbling through your entire bead stash in search of decorative beads that will contrast in color and be just the right size to fit inside the chain loops. I do not recommend this approach unless you have an exceedingly large stash.]

Open Chain

The only real difference between this and a regular chain stitch worked in BCB style is the distance between where the needle comes up (A and C above) and where it comes down (B and D above). However, this makes quite a difference in the overall look of the stitch, as you'll see from the color pictures. To exaggerate the difference even more, string on 20 to 30 seed beads for each stitch – but don't use this for anything fragile or washable!

Beads Crossing Beads

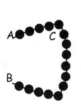

I'm going to show this with alternating black and white loops to help you visualize the stitch.

Loop 1: Bring up needle at A, string on 15-18 black seed beads, and bring needle down at B. A and B here should be at least 1/8 inch apart if not more. Bring up the needle for the next stitch at C.

Loop 2: With needle coming up at C, string on 15-18 white beads and bring needle down at D.

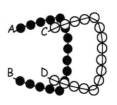

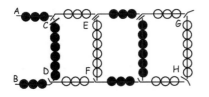

To end the chain, make two short stitches of 4-6 beads at the outer corners of the last loop, as shown at E and F at left.

Thread crossing thread

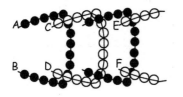

Bring needle up at A, string on 12 black beads, needle down at B. Remember to make the distance between A and B larger than for regular chain stitch, perhaps as much as a quarter of an inch. Come up at C and make a tiny stitch across the thread between beads 3 and 4, bringing the needle down outside the loop.

Bring needle up again at C, string on 12 white beads, and bring needle down at D. Come up at E and make a small stitch across the thread between beads 3 and 4, bringing the needle down outside the loop.

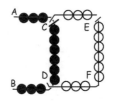

When you are ready to end the chain, take two small stitches across the thread between beads 3 and 4 and again between beads 9 and 10 of the last loop, as shown at G and H at left.

Open chain stitch is one variation where the TCT method really comes into its own. The neat, clear open squares it forms cry out for ornamentation. Here are some possibilities:

Use a bugle bead in the center row of beads. String (4sb, bb, 4sb) for each stitch.

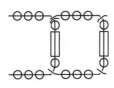

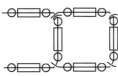

Use bugle beads on all three sides of the open square formed by each stitch. String (1sb, bb, 2ab, bb,2sb,bb, 1sb) for each stitch.

Put bugle beads on each side and a star bead in the center. String (sb, bb, 2sb, star, 2sb, bb, sb) for each stitch.

Work the stitch vertically with a dangle in the center of each row. (This is a tricky one and I wouldn't recommend trying it for your first variation.) For the version shown in the diagram, string on (6 sb, cube, sb). Using the last seed bead as a pivot, go back through the cube and 4 seed beads. Now string on 5 sb, bring needle down, take a catch stitch at one corner, and begin the next stitch.

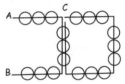

As you continue working, the dangles of later stitches will overlap those of earlier stitches.

The TCT version of open chain stitch also makes a good basis for working a raised chain band in a contrasting color (see raised chain band, below).

Stitch Back Through

Loop 1: Bring needle up at A, string on 9 beads, needle down at B. This will make a loose open loop but you need to visualize it as an open square to know where to start the next loop; lghtly drawn guidelines may be helpful.

Loop 2: Bring needle up at C, stitch back through beads 4-6, string on 9 beads, down again at C.

Loop 3: Bring needle up at D, stitch back through beads 4-6 of previous loop, string on 9 beads, down again at D. Note that while loop 2 began at the top of the stitch, loop 3 begins at the bottom of the stitch. Alternating beginning places in this way helps to keep the stitch better anchored to the cloth. Of course if for some reason you want the beads to flap freely you can begin each stitch at the top.

Continue in this fashion, starting loops alternately at the top and bottom. When you are ready to close, bring needle up at the appropriate corner of the last loop, stitch through the three middle beads, and bring needle down again, as shown at E and F above.

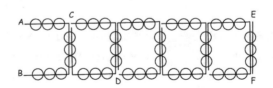

All the variations described for the TCT version of open chain stitch can also be worked with the SBT version.

Two-Bugle Chain Stitch

Beads Crossing Beads

String each loop in the sequence (1 sb, 1 bb, 8 sb, 1 bb, 1 sb). This makes a very tight stitch with the bugles splaying out from the beginning of the loop. To finish the chain, bring needle up inside the last loop, string on 4-6 seed beads and bring needle down outside the loop, as shown at E and F.

For a more open stitch, try the sequence (2 sb, 1bb, 8 sb, 1 bb, 2 sb)

Stitch Back Through

Loop 1: Bring needle up at A, string on (1 sb, 1bb, 3sb, 1bb, 1sb), bring needle down at B.

Loop 2: Bring needle up at C. Pass through the middle seed bead of the previous loop, string on the same sequence of beads (1 sb, 1bb, 3sb, 1bb, 1sb), and bring needle down at C again.

When you are ready to end the chain, bring the needle up beside the middle seed bead of the last loop, stitch through that bead and bring the needle down again to anchor the last loop, as shown at D and E

Thread Crossing Thread

The TCT method isn't very interesting for this particular stitch variation, as it just looks like two lines of back stitch alternating bugles and pairs of seed beads, but here it is if you really want to do it:

Loop 1: Bring needle up at A, string (1 sb, 1bb, 2sb, 1bb, 1sb) and bring needle down at B, right beside A.

Loop 2: Bring needle up at C, inside the first loop, and bring thread across the thread between the two middle seed beads of that first loop. String (1 sb, 1bb, 2sb, 1bb, 1sb), cross the thread of the first loop again and bring needle back down again at C.

When you are ready to end the chain, bring a single stitch of thread (no beads) across the thread between the middle two beads of the last loop.

One-Bugle Chain Stitch

Beads Crossing Beads

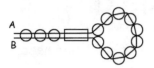

Loop 1: Bring needle up at A and string (3 sb, 1bb, 12 sb). Go back through the bb and the first 3 sb and bring the needle down at B.

Loop 2: Bring the needle up at C, inside the 12-bead loop just formed, and string (3 sb, 1bb, 12 sb). Go back through the bb

and the first 3 sb and bring the needle down at D.

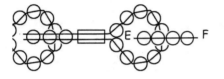

When you are ready to end the chain, bring the needle up inside the last loop, string 4-6 seed beads and bring it down outside the loop, as shown at E and F.

This makes an interestingly lumpy line alternating bugle beads with seed bead loops.

Stitch Back Through

Loop 1: Bring needle up at A. String (1 sb, 1 bb, 5 sb) and stitch back through (bb, 1 sb) to bring needle down at B.

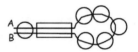

Loop 2: Bring needle up at C and pass through the third seed bead in the 5-bead loop of the previous stitch. String (1 sb, 1 bb, 5 sb) and stitch back through (bb, 1 sb) to bring needle down at D.

When you are ready to end the chain, bring needle up beside the middle bead of the last loop, pass through that bead and bring the needle down again, as shown at E and F.

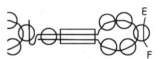

Thread Crossing Thread

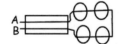

Bring needle up at A, string (1 bb, 4 sb). Go back through bugle bead and bring needle down at B.

Come up at C and repeat, coming down at D.

When you are ready to end the chain, bring the needle up at E, inside the last loop; cross the thread between beads 2 and 3 of the 4-bead loop and bring needle down at F on the outside of the loop.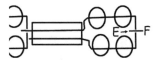

Raised Chain Band

[Note: Because this is rather a bulky stitch, I prefer to use Delicas or #13 beads rather than #11 seed beads for this stitch. If you are using #11 seed beads, use 5 to 6 beads for each stitch in the foundation ladder, 15 to 18 for the first raised chain stitch, and 20 to 22 for subsequent stitches.]

 Lay down a foundation ladder of parallel stitches, each comprising 7 to 8 beads, spaced approximately 4 mm apart.

Now work chain stitch over these base stitches: 12 to 14 beads in the first loop, 15 to 18 in subsequent loops.

 Alternatively, use bugle beads, buffered with a seed bead at each end, for your base ladder and work the chain over them.

Open chain stitch, worked TCT style with bugles (see above) also makes a good basis for the raised chain band.

Twisted Chain Stitch

This works best with either TCT or SBT techniques; it can be worked with BCB, but that's basically wasted effort as the characteristic twist is hardly perceptible among the piles of loops created with the BCB method.

Whether using TCT or SBT, you will want to make your starting and ending points (A and B) a little farther apart than for regular chain stitch, though not so far as for open chain. I find that having A and B about a bead's width apart works well; this comes naturally with the SBT technique but requires a little extra thought with TCT.

Thread Crossing Thread

Bring needle up at A, string on 12-16 seed beads (just be sure it's an even number), and bring needle down at B. Now take the loose loop of seed beads you have just made and, holding the thread taut against the fabric with one hand, with the other hand pinch the top of the loop and twist it over once.

Bring needle up at C, inside the twist, and secure the loop with a small stitch crossing between the beads.

Normally, in TCT technique, you would start threading the beads for the next stitch as soon as you have brought your thread across the thread of loop AB. Because of the need to keep the start and end points slightly separate, I find it works better to work each TCT chain stitch as a detached stitch (see below), bringing the needle down just outside the loop as illustrated and starting the next loop slightly above C.

Stitch Back Through

Bring needle up at A, string on 11-15 seed beads (this time you want an *odd* number) and bring needle down at B. Bring needle up at C, just beside the middle bead of the loop. Now you want to string C the wrong way round. One way is to pinch the loop between the thumb and forefinger of your free hand and twist it, as you did for the TCT method. Another is to go *around* that middle bead and enter the hole from the side opposite that on which you brought up the needle. When you pull the needle through and the thread taut, the loop should automatically twist over on itself.

Lines or areas filled with this stitch have a beautiful textured quality.

Twisted Chain Stitch with 2 Bugles

This can be worked with either the SBT or the TCT technique. In either case it tends for a highly textured, slightly awkward stitch with the two bugle beads crossing each other; take a look at the color pictures and try a

sample before deciding to spend a lot of time with this stitch. Some people like the "pick-up-sticks" look of the crossed bugle beads and some find it drives them crazy.

It's a good idea to buffer your bugle beads with several seed beads at each end, to give the stitch some flexibility; this means that even with short (3-4.5mm) bugles it's going to be a very long stitch indeed.

Twisted Chain Stitch with 1 Bugle

Worked with care to keep the one bugle bead on the underneath side of the twisted chain, this is a very much easier stitch to work than the two-bugle version. To make sure your bugle bead winds up on the underside, always string it early in the sequence (here

the stringing sequence is (sb, bb, 10 sb) and be sure to twist the bottom half of the stitch up and over the top half before taking the thread crossing stitch that anchors it.

Twisted Chain Stitch with E Bead

Worked in SBT style, and taking care to keep the stitches close together, this produces an effect as if the two seed bead sides of the stitch wrap around the larger bead. Using a 6/0 or larger central bead forces the ends of the stitch away from each other and adds to the rounded, nesting effect; you can see this more clearly in the color picture than in the diagram.

Double Chain

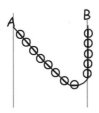

This is one variation where the TCT method is quite useful. It may be helpful to draw two light parallel guide lines on your fabric before starting. Bringing needle up at A, string on as many seed beads as necessary to make a nice generous loop before you bring the needle down at B. Ok, if you want numbers, I've shown a loop of 13 beads with 8 beads crossing diagonally and the other 5 hanging down straight (they'll be pulled into this position by the next loop), but that's MY beads and MY stitch. Be prepared to fiddle around a little bit to find out what size of stitch is comfortable for you and how many beads that takes with the beads you're using. MAKE SAMPLES!

Come up at C, slightly inside the guideline; cross thread of previous loop where there are just enough seed beads between B and C to make a straight line along the guideline. In this diagram, that would be between beads 8 and 9 of the first loop. Thread on the same number of seed beads as before (13,

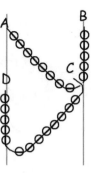

if you insist on slavishly following the diagram) and come down at D.

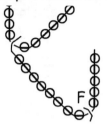

Bring needle up at E, cross threads and continue as before. When you are ready to stop, hold down the last loop with a short straight stitch as shown at F at left.

Okay, I know this has required a fair amount of guesstimating numbers of seed beads on your part, but there really isn't any short answer; it all depends on the size of your beads, how far apart your guidelines are drawn, and how deep you want the loops to be.

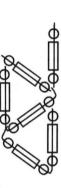

Another way to get the feel of the stitch is to work it with bugle beads, stringing (sb, bb, 2sb, bb, sb) for every loop. In this case, though, you can't start with drawn guidelines, because the length of the bugle beads will define how far apart your lines can be and how deep the loop is.

If you do this with long bugle beads that leave plenty of room in the middle, you can further ornament the stitch by working a zigzag chain band over the diagonal bugle beads. (See color pictures for an example.) Another possible ornamentation: end each loop with a long oval pearl or other decorative bead and a closing seed bead. The pearl and the two seed beads on either side of it will form the perpendicular lines of the stitch and the other seed beads will form the diagonal.

Obviously there are lots of other variations you can work with this stitch; as one of my math professors used to say when he didn't want to go through the tedious details, the proof is left as an exercise for the reader. (That's you. Go think up a variation.)

Detached Chain Stitch

As with regular chain stitch, there are three ways you can work it: beads crossing beads, thread crossing thread, or stitching back through the center bead in the previous loop. Any of these will work; it depends on what you want the finished look to be. For detailed instructions, look back to the BCB, TCT and SBT instructions for beginning and finishing chain stitch.

Beads Crossing Beads

 ### Thread Crossing Thread

Stitch Back Through

.

Detached chain stitches offer endless possibilities for creative arrangement. This is just a beginning:

Detached chain stitches (bcb) arranged in a floral shape.

Detached chain stitches (sbt) filling a heart outlined in bugle and seed beads.

Detached chain stitches (sbt) arranged to form a heavy line.

Since each stitch stands on its own, rather than being looped through the previous stitch, you have the option of beginning the loop with a sequin or decorative bead (E bead, Miyuki cube or triangle, 3-4 mm crystal, small pearl, etc.)

 If working the detached chain in bcb style, you can also end the stitch that holds the loop down with a sequin or decorative bead.

Staggered loops of sbt chain stitch with sequins make a nice broad line.

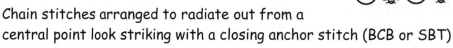

Chain stitches arranged to radiate out from a central point look striking with a closing anchor stitch (BCB or SBT) that ends with a sequin.

Color Shifting With Chain Stitch

Using the BCB method, you can get very interesting raised chains with a braided look by stringing each stitch with varying colors of beads. Here are some simple color variations to try.

Stripe

String (seven black beads, 7 white beads). The first stitch looks like this. A line of stitches shows the stripe effect. For the example in the color pictures, I used silver-lined green and matte bronze beads.

Checkerboard

Again, use two contrasting colors and string as for the stripe, only reversing colors every two stitches, so that your stringing sequences look like this:

Stitch 1: (7 white, 7 black)
Stitch 2: (7 white, 7 black)
reverse
Stitch 3: (7 black, 7 white)
Stitch 4: (7 black, 7 white)
reverse

Stitch 5: (7 white, 7 black)
Stitch 6: (7 white, 7 black)
...and so on.
The example in the color pictures section is worked with silver and blue beads.

Triple braid

This time choose 3 colors that contrast both with each other and with your background fabric. Finding a nice set of contrasting beads that are all more or less the same size can be quite a challenge, especially if you're undisciplined like me and buy anything from 9's to 14's, plus delicas, whenever you see a hank in colors you like. So you may have to go to the bead store to fill out your stash for this one.

Ok, say you've got your three colors. Since I was working all these examples on lavender cloth, I used matte purple, luster green and opalescent white, but for these diagrams we're stuck with black, grey and white. The stringing sequence is a strict alternation of black, grey, and white, using only 7 beads in each color, so that each stitch contains two colors of beads, as follows:

     Stitch 1: (7 black, 7 white)

Stitch 2: (7 grey, 7 black)

   Stitch 3: (7 white, 7 grey)

And that's it. Stitches 4, 5 and 6 are the same as 1, 2 and 3; you just keep repeating the sequence over and over and you'll get a fantastically complicated-looking triple braid.

It's worth experimenting with different colors here; I tried the same sequence substituting galvanized raspberry for the opalescent white, and got a much more dramatic effect.

Inside out

 Take two contrasting colors – for the diagram and instructions, of course, we'll use black and white. String (3 white, 8 black, 3 white) on each stitch.

Close the line of stitching with an anchor stitch of 4-6 black beads.

Since the beginning and ending beads of the BCB chain stitch are in the middle of the line of stitching you create, the white beads overlay the black ones so that the black is only partially visible along the outside edges and the very end of the stitching. If you substitute green and a floral color such as bright pink (in the color pictures you will see that I used green and purple) you get the effect of a green vine with purple berries peeking out from the foliage.

A long undulating line of these stitches, with chains branching off here and there, would make a great dangling vine motif for crazy quilting!

Outside in

If you want the look of little flowers framed by foliage, start and end your stitch with 3 beads of a flower color and use green for the middle beads; in the picture I used (3 pink, 8 green, 3 pink). To maintain the framing effect I began with a single stitch of (14 green) before starting with the pink beads, and I closed the line with a single stitch of (5 green).

Obviously you can play with color variations like these forever! Try doing the last version with a different warm color in each stitch – pink, orange, rose, burgundy. Try working the checkerboard by reversing colors every stitch instead of every two stitches. Maybe there's a four-color braid hiding somewhere in your bead stash; see how many colors you can use before it looks like a random mess.

CHAPTER SIX: CHEVRON STITCH

Basic Chevron Stitch

 In traditional embroidery this is a simple stitch rather than a complex one, because the horizontal and diagonal stitches don't overlap.

It can be worked in beads this way, as a variation of back or satin stitch. However, working it as a compound stitch with the TCT method helps to keep the horizontal bead lines in place and also offers some interesting variations.

It helps to draw two light parallel lines on your fabric as guidelines to keep the stitch even.

Thread Crossing Thread

Bring the needle up at A, string four seed beads, and down at B.

Come up at C, draw thread over between beads 2 and 3 of previous stitch, string 4-8 seed beads (exactly how many you need depends on how far apart your lines are and what size beads you are using) and bring the needle down at D.

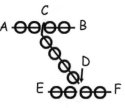 Bring needle up at E, string four seed beads, and down at F.

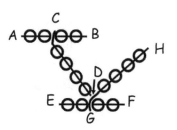

Bring needle up at G, draw thread over between beads 2 and 3 of previous stitch, string 4-8 seed beads, and come down at H.

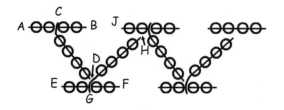 Bring needle up at J to start the next horizontal line of four seed beads on the top row.

Chevron Stitch with Bugles

Work just as regular TCT chevron stitch, except instead of stringing seed beads for the diagonal stitches, use a sequence of (sb,bb, sb).

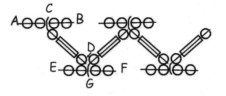

Chevron Stitch with Sequins or Decorative Beads

Work as basic TCT chevron stitch, except that you begin and end each of the parallel stitches with a sequin, so the stringing sequence is (seq, 4sb, seq). Instead of a sequin you can use a decorative bead (E bead, Miyuki cube or triangle, 3-4 mm crystal, small pearl, etc.) Depending on the size of the bead and the sharpness of the edges, you may want to buffer the decorative bead with a seed bead after it.

Fly Stitch Chevron

All this requires is that you put on more beads for the "horizontal" stitches than you need to reach from A to B, so that you get a loop which can be pulled into a V instead of a straight line of beads.

If you use the same beads and guidelines, the same distance apart as you used in the basic stitch, all you have to do differently is string 8 beads for each "horizontal" stitch and bring up the thread for the diagonal stitch inside rather than on the guideline, so that it pulls the 8 beads into a V shape. Because this stitch is so symmetrical in appearance, it can be a bit confusing until you get used to the alternation of long and short stitches, so I'm going to walk you through two full repeats in the diagram.

Bring needle up at A, string (8 sb) and down at B, which should be close enough to A to allow the string of beads to fall in a gentle loop.

Bring the needle up at C, cross the thread of the previous stitch between the middle two seed beads, string (4 sb) and bring down at D.

Come up at E, string on (8 sb) and come down at F.

At this point there's nothing holding the loop EF in place, just as there wasn't anything holding the loop AB in place when you took your first stitch; but if you're working in the same direction as the diagram, EF will <u>feel</u> more unstable because it'll want to flop down like this:

NO

Don't let it do this! Hold it in place with your thumb, if necessary, while you bring your needle up at G, cross the thread of the previous stitch between the two middle seed beads, string (4 sb) and come down at H.

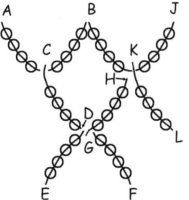

Ok, that's one full repeat. Now start the next repeat. Bring the needle up just beside B, string (8 sb) and come down at J.

Come up at K, cross the thread of the previous stitch between the two middle seed beads, string (4 sb), and come down at L.

Bring the needle up just beside F, string (8 sb) and come down at M.

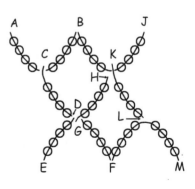

Come up at N, cross the thread of the previous stitch between the two middle seed beads, string (4 sb), and come down at P.

[TIP: Pay attention to the instructions! Don't try to do it just by looking at the last diagram! If you just look at the final diagram you might think that you bring your needle down at D and immediately up again at G. . Sometimes a broken line in a diagram indicates one thread *crossing over another, for instance where the thread C-D crosses over the loop A-B. Sometimes it indicates that you bring your needle down where the line breaks, as at D, and where the needle comes up again is the start of a completely different stitch (in this case, at E.)]*

Chevron Fly Stitch with Bugles

A beautiful and symmetrical stitch can be developed by using the stringing sequence (sb, bb, 2 sb, bb, sb) for each of the "parallel" stitches (now deep V shapes) and the sequence (sb, bb, sb) for the diagonal stitches. Except for the stringing sequences, this stitch is worked exactly like the basic Chevron Fly Stitch, so I won't diagram it in quite as much detail.

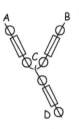

Bring needle up at A, string (sb, bb, 2sb, bb, sb) and down at B, which should be close enough to A to allow the string of beads to fall in a gentle loop. Bring the needle up at C, cross the thread of the previous stitch between the middle two seed beads, string (sb, bb, sb) and bring down at D.

Come up at E, string on (sb, bb, 2sb, bb, sb) and come down at F. Come up at G, cross the thread of the previous stitch between the two middle seed beads, string (sb, bb, sb) and come down at H.

Bring the needle up just beside B, string (sb, bb, 2sb, bb, sb) and come down at J. Come up at K, cross the thread of the previous stitch between the two middle seed beads, string (sb, bb, sb), and come down at L.

Bring the needle up just beside F, string (sb, bb, 2sb, bb, sb) and come down at M. Come up at N, cross the thread of the previous stitch between the two middle seed beads, string (sb, bb, sb), and come down at P.

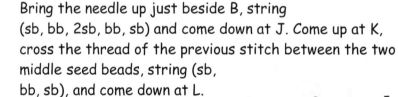

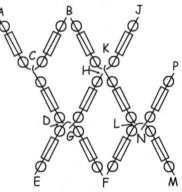

CHAPTER SEVEN: COUCHING

Popular in American Indian beadwork, where it is also known as "laid stitch", this consists of laying down a line of strung beads and then working back along the line to stitch the thread down (TCT) at intervals.

Bring needle up at A, string on 12 beads, bring needle, down at B. Come up at C and take a tiny, tight stitch crossing the thread between two beads. Come up again at E and do the same thing. Repeat couching as many times as necessary to hold down the line of beads.

This is an extremely flexible stitch; you can work spirals, curved lines, outline figures, etc; you can string on different colors and combinations of beads to add textural interest; you can cover areas with solid beadwork very quickly.

That being said - I don't use this stitch much except as an adjunct to satin stitch, because with a long line of beads I have trouble getting them to lie where I want them to be when I stitch them down, and with a short line I figure I can backstitch them almost as fast and have a much more secure piece of work. This is why you're getting only one crummy little picture of couched beadwork.

However, for those who get along well with this stitch, it can be a very quick and easy way to get a lot of beads on fabric fast.

CHAPTER EIGHT: CRETAN STITCH

Basic Cretan Stitch

In embroidery, this compound stitch is usually worked in an open style, so that the background fabric shows through. It works well as an open stitch in beadwork also, but it is possible to work the basic versions so close together that they create a dense, textured filling.

Beads Crossing Beads

Bring needle up at A, string on 9 beads, down at B. B should be close enough to A to let the loop of beads curve slightly. Now bring the needle up at C, string on 11 beads, draw beads down against the fabric (to prevent thread crossing thread instead of beads crossing beads), and bring needle down at D.

Bring the needle up at E, string on 11 beads again, draw them tight against the fabric, and stitch down at F.

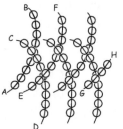

Continue in this way, beginning stitches alternately at the top and at the bottom of the broad line of beads you are forming. When ready to end the line, bring the needle up near the center of the line, string on 4-6 seed beads and secure the last 9-bead loop with a short stitch, as shown at G and H at right..

This produces an interesting stitch with a raised texture in the middle; the only thing wrong with it is that it doesn't actually look much like traditional Cretan stitch. Let's see how the other crossing methods do.

Thread Crossing Thread

Bring needle up at A, string on 9 beads, down at B. Come up at C, draw thread tight between beads 6 and 7 of the previous stitch, string on 6 beads and bring needle down at D.

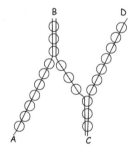

Come up at E, draw thread tight between beads 3 and 4 of the previous stitch, string on 6 beads and bring needle down at F.

Continue until you are ready to end the line, then anchor the last loop with a small stitch crossing the thread between beads 3 and 4, as shown at G and H at right.

That's a little better, but it still creates curves leaning in the direction of stitching.

Stitch Back Through

Bring needle up at A, string on 9 beads, down at B. Take a tiny stitch, come up right beside B, and stitch back through the last 3 beads of the previous stitch; string on 6 beads and bring needle down at C.

Take a tiny stitch and come up right beside C. Stitch back through the last three beads of previous stitch, string 6 beads, and bring needle down at D.

Take a tiny stitch and come up beside D; stitch back through the last three beads of previous stitch, string 6 beads, bring needle down at E.

By now you should see how each stitch straightens out the last three beads of the previous one by pulling them down and out in the direction of stitching.

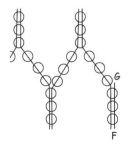

Continue in this manner until you are ready to stop the line. For a nice looking finish that keeps the last 3 beads of the last stitch perpendicular to the line, bring needle up near the end of the last stitch, stitch through three beads, pull them out to the desired positon, and stitch down, as shown at F and G

.You can clean up the first stitch in the same way. I didn't mention this in the starting instructions because you had enough to think about already, but now that you know how the stitch ought to look, try beginning like this:

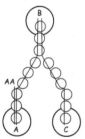

Bring needle up at A, string on 9 beads, and bring needle down at B, leaving a little slack in the loop of beads. Go back and bring needle up at A again; string through the first three beads of the previous stitch, pull them perpendicular to your planned line of stitching, and bring needle down at AA. Now when you finish your whole line of stitching will be beautiful and symmetrical.

I find this the easiest way to produce an even Cretan stitch with the characteristic curves looking nice and symmetrical, and it's the technique used in the variations discussed below.

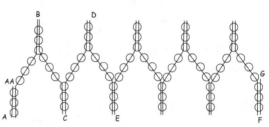

Cretan Stitch Sequin or Decorative Bead Points

Bring needle up at A, string on (sequin, 9 sb, sequin), down at B. To straighten out the first 3 beads, bring needle up again at A, pass through the first 3 beads, and bring down at AA.
Bring needle up again at B, go back through the sequin and then through beads 9 - 7 of previous stitch, string on (6 sb, sequin), down at C.

Take a very small stitch and bring needle up through sequin at C, then through beads 6- 4 of previous stitch, string (6 sb, sequin), down at D. Continue this way until you are ready to end the line, then close it with a short stitch through the last 3 beads and sequin of the last stitch.

Instead of a sequin you can use a small decorative bead (E bead, Miyuki cube or triangle, 3-4 mm crystal, small pearl, etc.) Depending on the size of the bead and the sharpness of the edges, you may want to buffer the decorative bead with a seed bead after it.

Cretan Stitch Bugle Bead Points

Use bugle beads at beginning and end of stitch, buffered as always by seed beads.

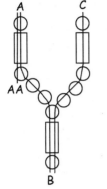

Bring needle up at A, string on (sb, bb, 5 sb, bb, sb), and come down at B. To straighten out the first 3 beads, bring needle up again at A, pass through the first 3 beads, and bring down at AA. Take a tiny stitch and come up right beside B. Stitch back through the last (sb,bb,sb) of the previous stitch. String (4 sb,bb,sb), and bring needle down at C.

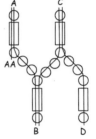

Come up just beside C, stitch back through the last (sb, bb, sb) of previous stitch, string on (4 sb, bb, sb), and bring needle down at D.

Continue this way until you are ready to end the line, then close it with a short stitch through the last 3 beads of the last stitch.

Cretan Stitch with Dangles

Bring needle up at A, string on (16 sb, bb, sb). Using the last seed bead strung as a pivot bead, go back through bugle bead and 7 seed beads, then bring needle down at B. To straighten out the first 3 beads, bring needle up again at A, pass through the first 3 beads, and bring down at AA. Bring needle up again at B. Pass needle through last three beads of previous stitch, string on 6 sb, and bring needle down at C.

Continue this way until you are ready to end the line, then close it with a short stitch through the last 3 beads of the last stitch

(Note: the example on the color pictures page shows a shorter bugle bead dangle, with just 1 seed bead before the bugle instead of 7.)

Any decorative bead will do, of course – a small pearl, a crystal, a Miyuki cube or triangle – or you can make the dangle with no large beads at all. Any stringing sequence you like is ok, as long as you end with a pivot bead.

Color/Value Gradation Within Cretan Stitch

Choose a series of 3 seed beads of the same size and color family but varying in value: for purposes of stitch description, let's call the values l (light), m (medium) and d (dark). If you prefer to work with different colors than with different values of the same color, then pick three colors that contrast well enough with each other to stand out and arbitrarily call them l, m, and d. Picking three colors adjacent to each other on the color wheel, such as blue, turquoise, and green, gives a smooth blending effect; picking three colors more widely spaced around the color wheel, such as red, blue, and gold, gives strong striped bands.

Bring needle up at A, string on 9 beads in the sequence (3l, 3m, 3d) , down at B. To straighten out the first 3 beads, bring needle up again at A, pass through the first 3 beads, and bring down at AA Bring needle up again at B, pass needle through last 3 beads of previous stitch, string on 6 beads in the sequence (3m, 3d), and bring needle down at C.

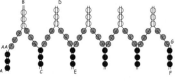

Try to work a long enough line of these stitches for the shading differences to show up as separate bands.

There are infinitely many variations on this theme, and nearly all of them are interesting. Try using more than three values, or contrasting silver-lined beads with matte, or using colors instead of values. Make the initial stitch of 9 beads, or 12, or 14, whatever suits your pattern.

This can be worked in the beads-crossing-beads style too, but the striping effect is not so clear.

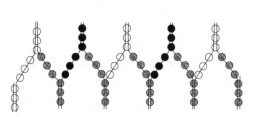

Color/Value Gradation Between Cretan Stitches

Using the same 3 values of seed beads as in the previous example, this time work each stitch in just one value, changing from light to dark as you go. (If you prefer to work with different colors, see color suggestions in previous section.)

Stitch 1: string 9 light beads
Stitch 2: 6 medium beads
Stitch 3: 6 dark beads
Stitch 4: 6 medium beads
Stitch 5: 6 light beads
and so on.

Threaded Cretan Stitch

First work a row of plain Cretan stitch. Be sure to use beads with big holes; you'll see why in a minute.

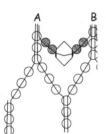

Now start a new thread. Bring the needle up at A, pass down through the first bead, thread on 3 to 7 seed beads in a contrasting color (however many it takes to fit between points) and pass back up through the first bead of the next point, bringing the needle down at B. If you use one or two more beads than the minimum required to fit between points, a graceful loop is formed.

Take a very tiny back stitch and come back up right beside B. Pass needle down through the same bead you just passed through, string on 3 to 7 seed beads, pass needle up through the first bead of the next point and bring needle down at C. (Now you see why you should have used Delicas to work the base row of Cretan stitch. After A, each point bead is going to have thread passing through it four times. Well, I did try to warn you!)

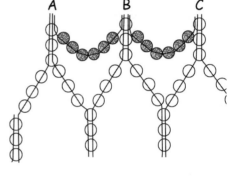

Once you get used to it, this is a marvellously versatile embellishment to the basic Cretan stitch. You can play with it all sorts of ways: try replacing the center beads of each loop with a crystal....

or a mini-dangle.....

or play with color and value changes to mimic the main stitch....

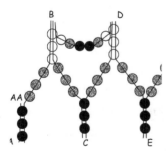

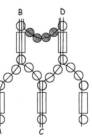

or combine it with one of the other variations, such as bugle bead Cretan stitch.

In short – as I said – the possibilities are endless. Go and have fun!

CHAPTER NINE: FEATHER STITCH

Basic Feather Stitch

This is an easy, versatile open compound stitch that's good when you don't need to completely cover the surface of your work.

Thread Crossing Thread

Bring needle up at A, string 8 beads (or any even number), bring needle down at B. Bring needle up again at C, draw the thread across between the 4th and 5th beads of the previous loop; string 8 beads and bring

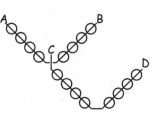

needle down at D, forming a new loop.

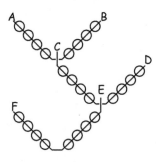

Bring needle up at E, draw the thread across between the 4th and 5th beads of the previous loop; string 8 beads and bring needle down at F.

When you are ready to close the line of stitching, bring the needle up just inside the last loop, between the 4th and 5th beads, cross the thread at that point and stitch down immediately, as shown at G and H at right.

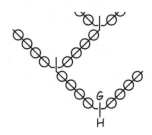

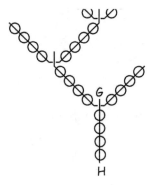

Alternative closure: bring needle up at G, cross thread of previous loop, string on 4 seed beads and bring needle down at H as at left.

With rocailles, this makes a neat, tight feather stitch that lies flat on the cloth. 2-cuts give a chunkier effect that I rather like, sharp and angular like some kind of coral.

Stitch Back Through

Bring needle up at A, string 7 beads (or any odd number), bring needle down at B. Bring needle up again at C, pass through the 4th bead of the loop just formed; string 7 beads and bring needle down at D, forming a new loop.

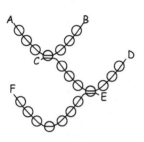

Bring needle up at E to begin the next loop; pass through the 4th bead of the previous loop, string 7 beads and bring needle down at F.

Note that you always bring the needle up on the side of the bead *away* from the direction you plan to stitch in, so that as it comes through the middle bead of the previous loop it's pointing in the right direction for the next loop.

When you are ready to close the line of stitches, bring needle up on one side of the middle bead in the last loop, pass through that bead and bring needle down immediately on the other side, as shown at G and H at right.

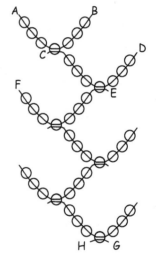

[TIP: With just seven beads it's pretty easy to keep track of the middle bead. If you go for a longer loop, say thirteen to fifteen beads, it's harder to be sure you're going back through the right bead. If this is a problem, try making the middle bead a different color, finish or size from the rest of the loop. Not only does it make the stitch easier but it adds a pretty accent.]

Beads Crossing Beads

Unlike the previous two methods, this makes a highly textured stitch with the beads of each loop rising as they cross over the previous loop and sinking back down against the fabric at the beginning and end of the loop, so what you get is a meandering raised line of beadwork that's highest in the middle. If you try to do it with only a few beads it can look lumpy; if you are generous with the beads on each loop it can make graceful curves.

Bring needle up at A, string 12 beads (or any number you're comfortable with; in this method it's not important exactly how many beads you string), bring needle down at B.

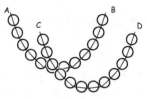

Pull the thread tight against the fabric, so that there are no gaps in the loop of beads you've just formed. It may help to hold the thread under the fabric down with your thumb while you bring your needle up again at C. String 12 beads and bring needle down at D, forming a

new loop whose beads cross over the beads of the first loop.

Pull the thread through the fabric tightly at D, so that there are no gaps between beads in this loop, and bring needle up at E. String 12 beads and bring needle down at F.

To close this stitch, come up at G, string at least four beads, cross the previous loop of beads and come down at H.

Bugle Beads Feather Stitch

Thread Crossing Thread

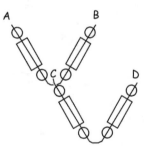

Bring needle up at A, string (sb, bb, 2 sb, bb, sb) and bring down at B. Bring needle up at C, cross the thread of the previous loop between the two middle seed beads. String (sb, bb, 2sb, bb, sb) and bring needle down at D, being careful to keep all your beads on the far side of the previous loop.

As you see, you need the 2 seed beads in the middle so the thread can cross between them. You really don't want to form this stitch with two bugle beads in the middle because your threads will be pulled taut

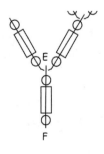

against the sharp ends of the bugle beads.

Continue until you are ready to close the line of stitching. You can do this with either of the methods described for the basic TCT feather stitch; my preference here is to use the second method and create an anchor stitch exactly like one half of the preceding stitches. Bring needle up at E, cross thread between the middle seed beads of the last loop, and string on (sb, bb, sb) before bringing needle down at F.

Stitch Back Through:

You need a minimum of one seed bead between the bugle beads, to be your bead that you stitch back through. The stitch will look smoother if you use three or five seed beads between the bugle beads, but the more seed beads you add, the less prominent the bugle beads are. It's a tradeoff; your choice. The instructions and diagram are for the minimum stringing sequence required.

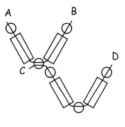

Bring needle up at A, string (sb,bb,sb,bb,sb) and bring needle down at B. Bring needle up at C and pass through middle seed bead of previous loop. String (sb, bb, sb, bb, sb) and bring needle down at D.

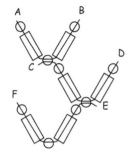

Bring needle up at E and pass through middle seed bead of previous loop. String (sb, bb, sb, bb, sb) and bring needle down at F.

Continue until you are ready to end the line of stitching; then bring needle up close to one side of the center seed bead of the previous loop, pass through that bead and bring needle down immediately on the other side, as shown at G and H at right.

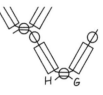

Beads Crossing Beads:

It's possible to work this bugle bead stitch with the BCB technique, but you have to be willing to string longer loops because you really have to have seed beads in the middle of the loop (where it bends) and at the beginning of the loop (where the string of beads bends again to cross over the previous loop).

The first stitch uses fewer seed beads than subsequent stitches, because at the very beginning you don't have the problem of crossing over a previous loop.

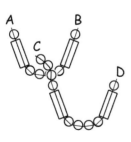

Bring needle up at A, string (sb, bb, 4sb, bb, sb) and bring needle down at B. Bring needle up at C, well inside the loop just formed. String (4sb, bb, 4sb, bb, sb) and bring needle down at D. Use this stringing pattern (4sb, bb, 4sb, bb, sb) for all subsequent stitches until you are ready to end the line; then bring needle up at E, string on 4 seed beads, and bring needle down at F to hold the last loop in place.

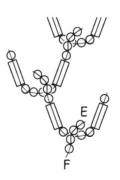

Extended Bugle Bead Feather Stitch

Any of the three crossing methods can be used here; I'm going to go through the TCT version in detail because that's the one I like best. If you've been following the feather stitch variations up to now, it shouldn't be difficult to see how the SBT and BCB versions work.

Thread Crossing Thread

Bring needle up at A, string the pattern (sb-bb-2sb-bb-sb), bring needle down at B and come up at C, crossing thread between the two middle seed beads of the first loop. For the second loop, string (sb, bb, 2 sb, bb, sb,bb, sb) and bring the needle down at D. Notice that here D is higher than C. The "bottom" of the loop should still be where the two seed beads are strung together; the arms are of different lengths.

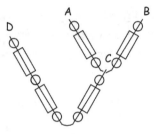

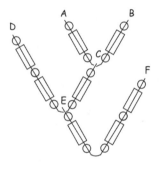

Come up at E, cross thread between the two seed beads, string (sb, bb, 2 sb, bb, sb,bb, sb) again and bring needle down at F.

Continue until you are ready to end the line of stitching; then bring needle up just inside the last loop and either take a tiny stitch across the thread to hold down that last loop, or cross the thread and add (sb, bb, sb) before bringing the needle down again.

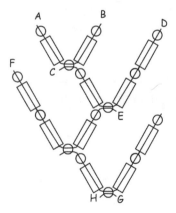

Stitch Back Through:

Work and close as for SBT bugle feather stitch, except that each loop after the first is strung (sb, bb, 2sb, bb, sb, bb, sb).

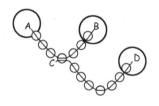

Beads Crossing Beads:

Work and close as for BCB bugle feather stitch, except that each loop after the first is strung (4sb,bb,4sb,bb,sb,bb,sb).

Sequin or Decorative Bead Feather Stitch

One way to accent the ends of the stitch is to put a sequin or a decorative bead at the end of each "arm." This time I'll work through the SBT method in detail and give a briefer description of TCT and BCB.

Stitch Back Through

For first loop, bring needle up at A, string (seq, 7sb, seq) and bring needle down at B. [If you are using large sequins you may want to use 9 or even 11 seed beads so that the stitch doesn't feel too crowded.]

Bring needle up at C, pass through the middle bead of the previous loop, string (7sb, seq) and bring needle down at D.

Bring needle up at E, pass through the middle bead of the previous loop, string (7sb, seq) and bring needle down at F.

Continue until you are ready to close the line of stitches;

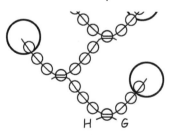

then bring needle up at G, pass through the middle of the previous loop, and bring needle down immediately at H.

Instead of a sequin you can use a small decorative bead (E bead, Miyuki cube or triangle, 3-4 mm crystal, small pearl, etc.) Depending on the size of the bead and the sharpness of the edges, you may want to buffer the decorative bead with a seed bead after it.

Beads Crossing Beads:

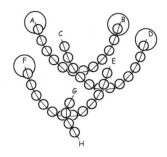

For first loop, string (seq, 12 sb, seq). For subsequent loops, string (12 sb, seq). Anchor with a short loop of 4-6 seed beads.

Thread Crossing Thread:

For the first loop, string (seq, 8sb, seq). For subsequent loops string (8sb, seq).

Variations on Feather Stitch Variations

All these variations can be combined and changed in creative ways to produce your own unique stitches.

Try working a feather stitch with short "branches" of seed beads and long "branches of alternating bugles and seed beads.

Work zigzag lines of feather stitch back and forth across your fabric...

...possibly tipping each line with a different bead or sequin.

Color-Tipped Feather Stitch

An easy way to accent the ends of the stitch is to use light value seed beads for the ends and dark value seed beads for the center.

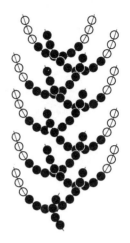

The diagram shows how to do this using the BCB method. String the first loop with 12 light seed beads. For the second loop, string 6 dark and 6 light beads. Continue to string first 6 dark and then 6 light beads for each subsequent loop, because with feather stitch you are always (after the first loop) working from the center to the outside.

Value Gradation Between Feather Stitches

If you have a good stash of beads in a particular color family, try working a series of loops from light to dark: first loop light beads, second loop medium, third and fourth loops dark, fifth loop medium, sixth and seventh loops light, and so on. The TCT version is shown here; SBT works much the same way; BCB tends to blend the values more evenly with the loops of beads crossing over beads.

The more values you can get into the gradation series, the more interesting the overall stitch looks.

Value Gradation Within Feather Stitch

Try shading the colors from light to dark and back again within each loop. The TCT method is illustrated, but SBT also works well. This particular variation tends not to look so good with the BCB method because the central and darkest beads of each loop are obscured by the light beads of the next loop passing over them.

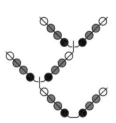

Mandala

This is one of my favorite things to do with the many variations of feather stitch.

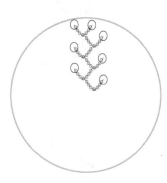

Just draw a rather large circle (4-6" diameter) lightly on your fabric with some erasable medium like a quilters' marking pencil and start working a feather stitch variation from the outside in towards the center.

Rotate the circle 90 degrees and work the same stitch again....

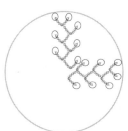

and again and again.

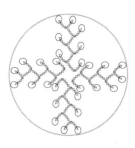

Now pick another variation and use it to fill in the open spaces left by the first stitch. Towards the center you'll actually be laying the new beads over the first layer of stitching.

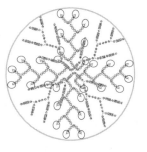

Now pick a third feather stitch variation and work it into the remaining gaps. You'll probably have to stop these lines of stitching well before you get to the center of the piece because it will be very crowded in there. Once you've filled the circle with as many lines of different feather stitches as you can, erase the guideline and you're left with a beautiful branching form.

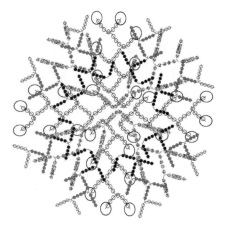

In Chapter 18 (Projects) you can see examples of this stitch form on the Feather Stitch Round Box, the Hands Wallhanging and on Triptych.

CHAPTER TEN: FERN STITCH

This can be worked as a simple stitch, with each step in making the "fern" shape independent of the other steps, so that you don't need to worry about any crossing methods. I prefer to use the SBT technique to make the stem part of the stitch, giving a smoother line; I'll describe both versions for the basic stitch. Whichever technique you use, this is a way to build a long line with short stitches branching out at regular intervals. This can be used as a linear stitch or shaped to fill a small area by varying the length of the branch stitches;it can be worked as an open stitch or very close, almost covering the area to be filled. You may find it helpful to pencil a line on your fabric showing where you want the stem of the fern stitch to lie, especially if you want an undulating or curved effect.

Basic directions are for the simplest version possible: straight stem, simple branches all the same length, one color of beads.

Open Fern Stitch

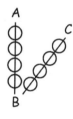

To begin the stem of the basic fern stitch, bring needle up at A, string on 4 beads, bring down at B. Take a ***very tiny*** back stitch and bring needle up just to the right of B; string on 4 beads and take needle back down at C.

Notice that C is somewhat lower on your fabric than A. You want to draw the beads of stitch AC out to form an acute angle with the beads AB, somewhere between 30 and 50 degrees. The farther C is from your stem line, the larger the angle will be; the larger the angle, the lower you'll have to place C. At the most extreme, you could make AC at right angles to AB, but this doesn't make a very interesting stitch, so let's stick with our acute angle for the time being.

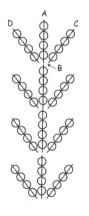

With another tiny stitch, bring needle up just to the ***left*** of B, string on 4 beads and take needle down at D.

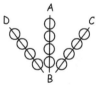

You have now completed one fern stitch – the stem and two branches. For the simple fern stitch, you just repeat this sequence over and over, beginning each new stitch at the bottom of the previous one.

Stitch Back Through version

For a more continuous stem look, you can bring the needle up for the second stitch between beads 2 and 3 of the previous stem stitch, at E.

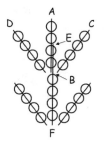

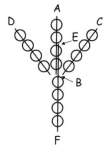

Pass back through beads 3 and 4, string on 4 new beads, and bring needle down at F.

Add two lines of beads branching out from F; work exactly as you worked the two previous branches, bringing the needle up on either side of F.

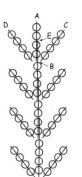

Continue making 4-bead stems and branches, beginning each stem by passing back through the last two beads of the previous stem.

Close Fern Stitch

By reducing the stem stitches to 2 beads, you can create a much denser looking stitch.

Fern Stitch with Bugle Bead Branches

Try using seed beads for your stem and bugle beads (buffered by seed beads) for the branches.

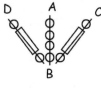

You begin exactly as with the basic open fern stitch: bring needle up at A, string on 4 beads, bring down at B. Take a *very tiny* back stitch and bring needle up just to the right of B. Now string (sb, bb, sb) and bring needle down at C.

Bring needle up again just to the left of B, string (sb, bb, sb) and bring needle down at D.

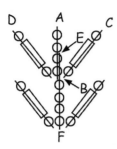

Notice that C and D may now be parallel with A or even higher than A, depending on the length of your bugle beads. I like to use a 4 to 4.5 mm bugle bead, so the stitch looks roughly like the diagram above.

Continue as for basic fern stitch (continuous line version): bring needle up at E, pass through last two beads of previous stem stitch, string on (4 sb) for next stem stitch, bring needle down at F and work bugle branches as above.

There are a number of easy variations within this theme. As long as your stem stitch is composed of seed beads, you can shorten it to (2sb) and work a very close stitch with bugles:

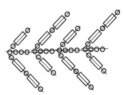

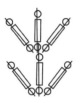

Alternatively, you can use the branch stringing sequence of (sb, bb, sb) for the stems as well, and produce a very symmetrical stitch.

You can double the length of every other branch to make an asymmetrical stitch:

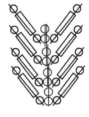

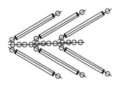

Or you can use extremely long bugle beads for the branches and produce an exaggerated stitch.

Fern Stitch with Sequin or Decorative Bead Branches

Bring needle up at A; string (sequin, 4sb) and bring needle down at B. (The example in the color pictures section is done with star-shaped sequins, so I'll use them in the diagrams here too.) Take a tiny stitch and bring needle up just to the right of B; string (4 sb, sequin) and bring needle down at C. Repeat on the left hand side of the stem stitch.

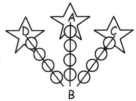

Continue as for basic fern stitch (continuous line version): bring needle up at E, pass through last two beads of previous stem stitch, string on (4 sb) for next stem stitch, bring needle down at F and work sequin-tipped branches as above. Instead of a sequin you can use a small decorative bead (E bead, Miyuki cube or triangle, 3-4 mm crystal, small pearl, etc.) Depending on the size of the bead and the sharpness of the edges, you may want to buffer the decorative bead with a seed bead after it.

Fern Stitch with Dangles

Instead of closing the branch stitches, end each one with a free-dangling bead: a 6/0 or E bead, a small pearl, a 4mm crystal or a small gemstone chip would work well here. If you want the dangles to be well separated, they must be very short, as in the instructions and diagram here; if you want to create a thick fringe of overlapping dangles on either side, you can make nice generous long ones.

Stem: Bring needle up at A, string on 4 beads, bring down at B.

First branch: Take a tiny back stitch and bring needle up just to the right of B; string on (5 sb, crystal, sb). Using the last seed bead as a pivot bead, go back through the crystal and one seed bead and take needle back down at C.

Second branch: Repeat steps for first branch, but this time working to the left of B and stitching down at D.

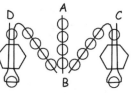

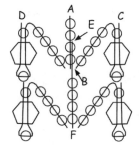

Bring needle up at E; pass through last two beads of previous stem stitch, string on (4 sb) and bring needle down at F for the second stem stitch.

Add branches with dangles as before.

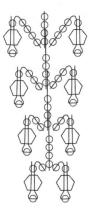

For a simple tapered motif, work four sets of stems and branches, with each set reducing the number of seed beads on the branches, as shown at right.

[Tip: As always when working dangles, don't pull the thread too tight. If you keep the tension tight, the "dangles" will not hang down as in the diagram but will sort of spray out from the ends of

the branches.]

Longer dangles will be more willing to swing freely. They will also have more tendency to overlap and wrap around each other.

Fern Stitch with Loop Dangles

This stitch is easier to follow if you use two different colors of beads; I'm going to call them "black" and "white", of course, but substitute any colors you like (just be consistent about it!)

Bring needle up at A, string on 4 black beads, bring down at B. Take a tiny stitch, come up just to the right of B, and string on (4 black, 6 white). Before bringing your needle down again, pass back through the first white bead you strung, as shown at right.

[Note: Making the loops this way will encourage them to lie flat on the fabric. If you'd rather have them pop out, then stitch back through the first white bead in the opposite direction, as shown at left.]

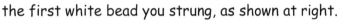

Now bring your needle down just inside the loop you've formed, at C.

Bring needle up just to the left of B and repeat on the left, bringing needle down at D:

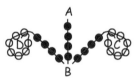

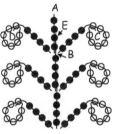

Bring needle up at E, pass through the last two beads of the previous stem stitch, and continue the sequence as above.

Fern Stitch with Detached Chain

Because fern stitch is a simple stitch, it's easy to combine with others – and once you start combining stitches, there's no end to the possible variations. This is just one combination that I came up with, using bugle beads in the stem and detached chain loops for the branches. I'm going to go through it in detail not because this particular combination in itself is so important, but to illustrate how you can combine stitches.

Bring needle up at A, string on (sb, bb, sb) and bring needle down at B. Bring needle up just to the right of B, as usual. Now, instead of stringing on some beads and bringing the needle straight down, you're going to work a ***detached chain stitch*** using the BCB technique. (If you'd rather practice this stitch in isolation first, refer to the instructions in the chain stitch chapter.)

String on (13 sb) and bring needle back down at B again, creating a loose flapping loop.

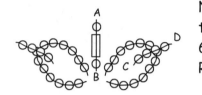

Now, to hold this loop down, bring needle up at C (inside the loop, near the outer edge of the stitch), string on 4 to 6 seed beads and bring needle down at D (outside the loop). Repeat on the other side of the bugle bead stem.

To begin the next stem-and-branches set, bring needle up at E, pass through the last seed bead of the previous stem stitch, string (sb, bb, sb) and bring needle down at F.

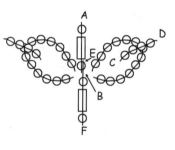

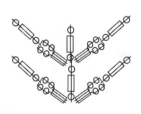

Work chain stitch branches as before.

You can probably see immediately how these two simple elements can be rearranged to make a whole group of different-looking stitches. You might work the detached chain stitches in TCT form and anchor them with (sb, bb, sb)

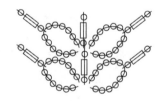

You could use the one-bugle chain stitch, TCT style, with the same bugle anchors.

Okay. I could go on and on, but you get the idea (I hope) and we probably can't spend the next year exploring all the possible ways to combine other stitches with Fern Stitch.

Color or Value Gradation Fern Stitch

I like to use value changes in this stitch, but you can also get an interesting effect by choosing three different colors of seed beads; just substitute those color names where I've used light, medium, and dark.

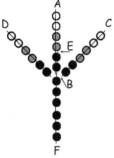

Select light, medium, and dark seed beads of the same size and hue.

Bring needle up at A, string (2 light, 2 medium, 2 dark) and bring needle down at B.

Take a very small stitch and bring needle up right beside B. String (2 dark, 2 medium, 2 light) and bring needle down at C.

Bring needle up just to the left of B and, again, string (2 dark, 2 medium, 2 light) before bringing needle down at D.

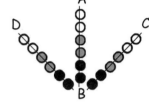

From here on all the stem stitches will be worked in dark seed beads, while the branch stitches will continue to be strung in the sequence (2 dark, 2 medium, 2 light).

Bring needle up at E, pass through the last two beads of the first stem stitch, string (6 dark) and bring needle down at F.

Now work two branches beginning on either side of F, stringing (2 dark, 2 medium, 2 light).

All subsequent stitches follow this pattern: string (6 dark) for the stem and (2 dark, 2 medium, 2 light) for each of the branches.

Shaped Fern Stitch

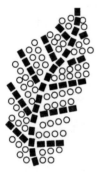

By varying the length of the branch stitches you can make a very graceful leaf or fern like shape. Penciled outlines are <u>very</u> helpful here. If you're working an open form and don't mean to go around the outside edge with more beading, use a white chalk pencil such as quilters use to mark quilting patterns so that the marks can be brushed off afterwards; or baste around the outside of the shape and pull the stitches out after beading.

Here's a nice simple leaf shape. The stem stitches will follow the center line. When working to fill a shape like this, the number of beads used in the stem and branch stitches depends on the width of the shape, how sharply it curves, and how tight you want to work the stitch. You can leave space between the stitches, like this:

Alternatively, pack the stitches tightly, working the stem and every third set of branch stitches in a contrasting color, to fill in a solid form.

CHAPTER ELEVEN: FISHBONE STITCH

This is technically a simple stitch in that no individual stitch has to loop around any previous stitch, but it does require careful placement of beads and stitches to be effective. At first glance it may look like a very closely worked fern stitch, but it's only the outlines of the work that are similar (and not necessarily those.) Ideally you want to achieve a sort of braided look running down the center of the beaded area, as you'll see in the following steps.

Basic Fishbone Stitch

As with shaped fern stitch, guidelines are very helpful in constructing the leaf-shaped fishbone stitch, so I'd sggest that you begin by drawing a leaf outline very lightly on your fabric.
Bring needle up at A (at the very tip of the leaf), string (2sb) and bring needle down at B on the spine of the leaf.
Bring the needle up at C on the right side of leaf outline, string (2sb) and bring needle down on the spine again, just below B.
Bring needle up at D, on left side of leaf, and string 2 or 3 seed beads – however many it takes to fill a straight line from D to the next open space on the spine.

These first two or three stitches are the hardest to fit correctly, so don't worry if they're a little uneven on your first try.
Keep on working diagonal lines of stitches down opposite sides of the leaf and you'll see the braided effect beginning to form. No exact count of beads for each stitch is possible, as it all depends on the size and shape of your beads and the size and shape of your drawing.

Worked in a solid color, this will give you a leaf-shaped form with subtle variations of shading as the light falls differently on the lines of beads running in opposite directions.

Veined Fishbone

Work pairs of stitches in contrasting colors to give the impression of veining.

Color Tipped Fishbone

To emphasize the outline, begin each stitch with one or two seed beads of a contrasting color to the main body. The example in the color pictures section uses iridescent orange and gold seed beads with matte green beads for the body of the leaf.

Open Fishbone

Space out your stitches so that the beads don't cover the ground solidly. This variation is probably how the stitch got its name; it really does look like a fish skeleton.

Broad Line Fishbone

If you start with one bead in each stitch, work the stitches close together, gradually work up to four or five beads in each stitch and from then on use the same number of beads in each stitch, rather than gradually increasing and decreasing them, you get a broad line with an interesting plaited look. The effect is very similar to Close Fly Stitch using the SBT technique (see Chapter 12)

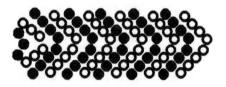

CHAPTER TWELVE: FLY STITCH

This is a compound stitch consisting of two single stitches. First you make a U- or V- shaped loop of seed beads, then you anchor it with one of the three crossing techniques.

Basic Fly Stitch

Thread Crossing Thread:

This is the version that looks most like traditional fly stitch, with a nice sharp V-shaped loop and an anchor stitch that lies flat on the fabric.

Bring needle up at A, string 8 or more seed beads (for a symmetrical stitch, you must use an even number of beads) and bring needle down at B. The distance between A and B is determined by the number and size of your seed beads; you want them to be close enough that when the loop is pulled tight it'll make a nice V shape enough space between the middle beads to draw a thread across, as right, and **not** a nearly flat line or a tight, narrow V that'll crowd the bottom beads.

with on

Bring needle up at C and pull thread across previous loop between beads 4 and 5. Either take a stitch down immediately (as at left) or add seed beads(any number will do) for the anchor stitch and bring the needle down where appropriate to fit the number of beads (as at right). The photographed sample shows the anchor stitch increasing from 0 to 3 seed beads and back down to 0.

Beads Crossing Beads:

As usual with BCB methods, this produces a compound stitch with a distinct raised texture.

Bring needle up at A, string 8 or more seed beads, needle down at B. The distance between A and B depends on how many seed beads you string on; you want it to be a nice generous loop like this.

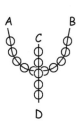

Bring your needle up at C, inside the loop you just made; string 4-6 seed beads and bring needle down at D, outside and below the loop, to hold it in place.

Stitch Back Through

If you're used to traditional embroidery, this will seem a very strange looking "fly stitch" indeed; it's something you literally cannot do with just needle and thread. The anchoring stitch is concealed in the middle bead of the loop, so you have a flat V shape with no "tail" of thread holding it down.

Bring needle up at A, string 9 or more seed beads (for a symmetrical stitch, you must use an odd number of beads) and bring needle down at B.

Bring needle up at C, go back through 5th bead of loop (or whatever your center bead is) and stitch down immediately at D.

Whichever crossing technique you use, since fly stitch consists of a single pair of stitches rather than a series of linked stitches like chain or feather stitch, you have a lot of freedom in the way you arrange the stitches; you can treat it as a linear stitch, horizontal

or vertical,

or scatter the stitches randomly to cover an area lightly

or arrange them to create different patterns.

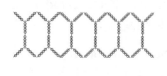

Fly Stitch with Bugle bead Loops

Thread Crossing Thread:

Bring needle up at A, string (sb,bb,2sb,bb,sb) and bring needle down at B.

For a symmetrical beaded anchor, bring needle up at C just inside the loop; draw thread across between the two middle seed beads; string (sb, bb, sb) and bring needle down at B.

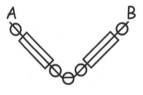

Beads Crossing Beads:

You'll probably want to have more seed beads in the middle of the loop this time, because you need them to make a graceful curve without any thread showing. Bring needle up at A, string (sb, bb, 4sb, bb, sb) and bring needle down at B.

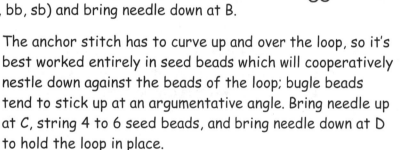

The anchor stitch has to curve up and over the loop, so it's best worked entirely in seed beads which will cooperatively nestle down against the beads of the loop; bugle beads tend to stick up at an argumentative angle. Bring needle up at C, string 4 to 6 seed beads, and bring needle down at D to hold the loop in place.

Stitch Back Through:

This time you want an odd number of seed beads between the two bugles in the loop. It can be done with just one bead, but I feel that 3 beads in the middle makes for a gentler and more attractive curve (not to mention less strain on the thread where it touches the possibly sharp edge of the bugle bead).

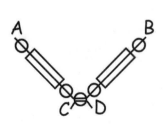

Bring needle up at A, string (sb, bb, 3sb, bb, sb) and down at B.

Bring needle up at C, pass through the middle bead in the loop, and bring needle down immediately at D.

Fly Stitch with Anchor Sequin or Decorative Bead

This must be worked in either TCT or BCB, as you must have an anchor stitch for the sequin! I'm going to give directions for TCT.

Bring needle up at A, string (8 sb) and bring needle down at B.

Bring needle up at C, just inside the loop, and cross the thread between beads 4 and 5 of the first stitch. String on (4 sb, sequin) and bring needle down at D. This anchor stitch holds the loop down at the top and the sequin down at the bottom. Instead of a sequin you can use a small decorative bead (E bead, Miyuki cube or triangle, 3-4 mm crystal, small pearl, etc.) Depending on the size of the bead and the sharpness of the edges, you may want to buffer the decorative bead with a seed bead after it.

This stitch variation lends itself nicely to circular motifs. You can work a series of fly stitches around a circle, all ending in the same sequin; do it casually and let the branches overlap...

...or fiddle with the stitch width and length until you can fill the circle evenly with no overlapping

Fly Stitch with Sequin or Decorative Bead Loop

This can be worked using any of the three crossing techniques; instructions and diagrams are for TCT method.

Bring needle up at A, string (sequin, 8 sb, sequin) and bring needle down at B. Bring needle up at C, inside the loop; cross threads between beads 4 and 5; string (4 sb) and bring needle down at D. Instead of a sequin you can use a small decorative bead (E bead, Miyuki cube or triangle, 3-4 mm crystal, small pearl, etc.) Depending on the size of the bead and the sharpness of the edges, you may want to buffer the decorative bead with a seed bead after it.

Obviously you can combine the sequin loop and sequin anchor to make a nice symmetrical stitch.

You can also combine sequins and bugle beads.

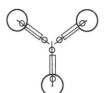

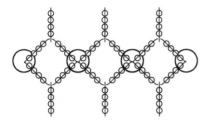

Sequin loop is another of those stitch variations that lends itself to interesting arrangements. On the color pictures page you will find a double row of fly stitches worked opposite each other, with the loop stitches in each row sharing sequins. The loops are worked with bronze metallic beads and the anchors with silver-lined glass beads.

Interlocking Fly Stitch

This works best with the TCT method.

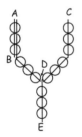

Loop 1: bring needle up at A, string 3 seed beads, bring needle down at B. Come back up at A, stitch back through first three seed beads, string 9 more, and bring needle down at C.

Come up at D, cross thread of first loop between beads 6 and 7, string three seed beads and bring needle down at E.

Loop 2: Bring needle up at C, stitch through the last three beads of the previous loop, string 9 seed beads and bring needle down at F.

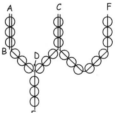

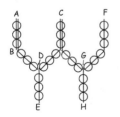

Come up at G, add 3 seed beads, bring needle down at H.

Begin the next loop by bringing the needle up at F and passing through the last three seed beads of the previous loop.

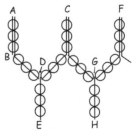

Continue until you are ready to end the line of stitching; then bring needle up at the upper point of the last loop, pass through the last three beads of that loop, and bring needle down immediately to hold these three beads in place, as shown at J and K.

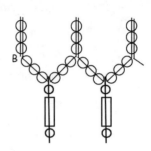

This stitch can also be worked with sequin or bugle points. On the color pictures page you will see a version done with seed stitch loops and bugle bead anchors.

Interlocking Circular Fly Stitch With Value Gradation

Select size 11 seed beads in dark, medium and light shades of the same color family.

Lightly pencil a small circle (about the size of a 35mm film canister). Mark center; divide circle into 8 segments. You will start and end each loop on a segment marker.

Loop 1: Bring needle up at A and string 3 dark, 6 medium, 3 dark seed beads; needle down at B. Bring needle up at C, cross thread between beads 6 & 7 of first stitch, and anchor with 3 to 6 light beads, whatever it takes to get to the center of your circle.

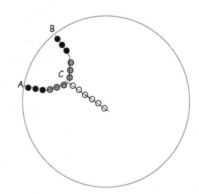

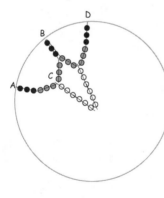

Loop 2 : come up at B, go through last 3 dark seed beads of previous loop; string 6 medium and 3 dark; down at D, anchor as in loop 1.

Continue working around the circle this way until you close the last loop by passing through the three dark beads of the previous loop, stringing on (6 medium), passing through the first 3 dark beads of A, and bringing the needle down at A. You will still need to take one more anchor stitch to hold this loop in place.

You can keep going in this way, stitching additional rows of fly stitch around the initial circle, to create a large and intricate mandala form.

Fly Stitch Dangles

These must be worked in TCT or BCB, since SBT does not allow for a beaded anchor stitch. Directions are for TCT method.

Loop: Bring needle up at A, string on (8sb), bring needle down at B.

Anchor: Bring needle up at C, inside the loop, and cross threads between beads 4 and 5.. String your dangle sequence – for purposes of this example, let's say it is (6sb, cube, sb). Using the last seed bead as a pivot, pass back through the cube and 5 seed beads and bring needle down at D, just outside the loop.

Close Fly Stitch

Work fly stitches in the SBT fashion very close together, producing a broad solid line.

This stitch has a tendency to try to flatten out as you work it.

One easy way to avoid this effect is to use a slightly larger bead for the center:

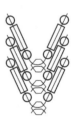

Close fly stitch can look very striking worked with bugle beads.

Double Reverse Fly Stitch

This consists of two fly stitches worked one over the other, the first one right side up and the second one upside down. I like to use the TCT technique for the anchor part of each stitch; the overlapping loops, however, naturally cross over each other in BCB style. If you're using very round beads, you may find that the second stitch will need 2-4 more beads than the first, because its loop has to go over the first one. The example was worked with Delicas, where the difference between stitches is negligible. Directions here are given using the same number of beads for each stitch; modify them if necessary.

I'm going to show the stitches worked alternately in white and black beads for clarity, but of course there's no reason you shouldn't work all the stitches in the same color or vary the colors in some other fashion. As we'll see, a very simple change in the color scheme can produce striking results with this stitch

The first stitch is worked in normal TCT fashion, using a relatively short anchor stitch:

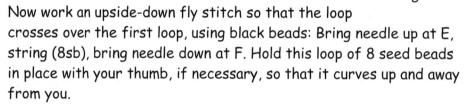

Bring needle up at A, string (8sb), bring needle down at B. Bring needle up at C, inside the loop; cross threads between beads 4 and 5, string (2sb) and bring needle down at D.

Now work an upside-down fly stitch so that the loop crosses over the first loop, using black beads: Bring needle up at E, string (8sb), bring needle down at F. Hold this loop of 8 seed beads in place with your thumb, if necessary, so that it curves up and away from you.

Now bring needle up at G – you will be coming up right beside the thread CD of the previous anchor stitch – cross between beads 4 and 5 of the black loop, string (2sb) and bring needle down at H.

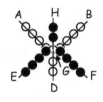

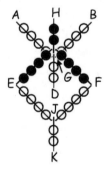

For the third stitch, use white beads again, and let the loop fall down (towards you). Bring needle up at E, string on (8sb), and bring needle down at F. Bring the needle up again at J, inside and above the white loop; cross threads between white beads 4 and 5, string (2sb) and bring needle down at K.

The fourth stitch goes upside down again. You may have to vary the length of the anchor stitches as you work to make them meet perfectly in the center.

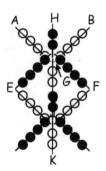

Braided Double Reverse Fly Stitch

In the diagrams above I showed all the right-side-up fly stitches (stitches 1 and 3) in white and all the upside down fly stitches (2 and 4) in black.

Suppose, instead of this scheme, you worked stitch 1 in white, stitches 2 and 3 in black, 4 and 5 in white, and so forth. Look what happens!

You get something that looks as if you have actually braided a white stitch and a black one together. Look at the color picture of this one; you can see the "braiding" effect more clearly there than in the diagram.

CHAPTER THIRTEEN: HERRINGBONE STITCH

Although this is a simple stitch in that each individual stitch stands alone without having to be held in place by anything else, the overall effect is of lines of beads overlapping each other, BCB style. It's possible to create very intricate color and texture variations but the stitch will not be completely flat.

The basic stitch can be a bit tricky to get started; it's important to get the spacing and angle of the individual stitches right. You might want to start by drawing two parallel guidelines on the fabric, about ¾" apart; you will be working up and down between these lines. To help you visualize the stitch I've shown all the "down" diagonal stitches in white, all the "up" ones in black. You might want to string two contrasting colors of seed beads the first time you try this stitch so that you can see what's happening better.

Open herringbone stitch

Bring needle up at A on the top line, string 10 (white) seed beads, down at B on the bottom line and make a small back stitch to come up at C. Note that C is not directly under A! String 10 (black) seed beads, bring needle down at D on the top line and make a small backstitch to come up at E.

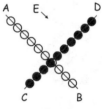

You now have a line of white seed beads slanting from A at upper left to B at lower right, crossed by a line of black seed beads slanting from C at lower left to D at upper right.

Starting at E, string 10 (white) seed beads, bring needle down at F on the bottom line and make a small backstitch to come up at G, between C and B.

Starting at G, string 10 (black) seed beads, bring needle down at H on the top line and make a small backstitch to come up at J, between E and D.

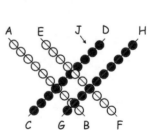

All this will probably give you the feeling of going two steps forward and one step back, which is indeed more or less what's going on, but once you get your intital spacing established and get into the rhythm the stitch goes quite quickly and makes a strong effect.

Closed Herringbone Stitch

An even stronger-looking stitch can be created if you bring the end points of the individual stitches together. This will require you to make stitches that are closer to vertical than those you made for closed herringbone – you want about a 60 degree angle from the guideline, not 45 degrees.

Most of the variations that follow will be illustrated with closed herringbone stitch.

Begin as with open herringbone:

Bring needle up at A on the top line, string 10 (white) seed beads, down at B on the bottom line and make a small back stitch to come up at C. *Note that C is not directly under A!* String 10 (black) seed beads, bring needle down at D on the top line and make a small backstitch to come up at E.

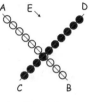

You now have a line of white seed beads slanting from A at upper left to B at lower right, crossed by a line of black seed beads slanting from C at lower left to D at upper right:

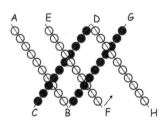

Starting at E, string 10 (white) seed beads, bring needle down at F on the bottom line, but *this time make your backstitch so that it comes up exactly at B.*

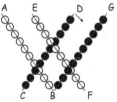

From here it gets easier as you will always be coming up at the end of an earlier stitch. String 10 (black) seed beads, bring needle down at G on the top line, and make a small backstitch to come up at D.

Now starting from D, string 10 (white) seed beads, bring needle down at H on the bottom line, and make a small backstitch to come up at F.

Sequin or Bead Edged Herringbone

Start and end each stitch with a sequin. The line of seed beads will hold the sequins in place. If you use large sequins and work the stitches even closer together than in the diagram, the sequins will overlap, giving an effect of an unbroken line of sequins defining the top and bottom edges of the stitch.

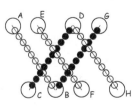

Instead of a sequin you can use a small decorative bead (E bead, Miyuki cube or triangle, 3-4 mm crystal, small pearl, etc.) Depending on the size of the bead and the sharpness of the edges, you may want to buffer the decorative bead with a seed bead after it.

Whipped Herringbone

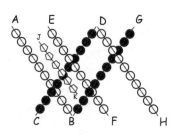

First, work a row of close herringbone stitch. You will begin whipping over the row between the first and second downward-slanting lines. Bring needle up at J, string on 6 seed beads, and bring it down again at K. The new line of seed beads will go over, or "whip," line CD.

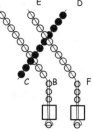

For the next line, come up inside the next closed diamond shape, at L. Again, string on 6 beads, and come down at M, whipping over line BG.

Herringbone Dangles

Bring needle up at A on the top line and string 10 (white) seed beads. Now, *before* you bring the needle down at B, you're going to add a short dangle. String on 3 more seed beads, a large decorative bead, and one last seed bead to act as a pivot. Bring your needle back through the large bead and the 3 seed beads. *Now* bring the needle down at B on the bottom line and make a small back stitch to come up at C.

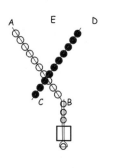

The next stitch is exactly the same as in the basic closed herringbone. String 10 (black) seed beads, bring needle down at D on the top line and make a small backstitch to come up at E.

Now, on the next downward stitch, add another dangle. Starting at E, string 10 (white) seed beads. String on 3 more seed beads, a large decorative bead, and one last seed bead to act as a pivot. Bring your needle back through the large bead and the 3 seed beads. Now bring the needle down at F on the bottom line and make a small back stitch to come up at B.

Continue in this manner, adding your dangle at the end of every downward-slanting stitch. Of course it doesn't always have to consist of three seed beads, a big bead and a pivot! You might want to create a dramatically long fringe with a dangle of 10 or more seed beads, or a textured dangle mixing seed, bugle and larger beads, or vary the dangle length from short to long along the line of stitchery, or use a charm as the pivot element at the end of each dangle. When we get to fringes, which will probably be in the next book after this one, you'll see even more ways to vary the dangle theme.

Internal Stripe Herringbone

You can create a stripe effect by stringing some of the internal beads on each stitch in a contrasting color. The diagram shows a simple sequence of (3 light, 4 dark, 3 light) in a ten-bead stitch. For the pictured sample I used an 11-bead stitch with the sequence (2 light, 2 medium, 3 dark, 2 medium, 2 light).

Herringbone Color Series I

Choose two contrasting colors and stitch the 1st, 4th, 7th and so forth stitches in color A, all others in color B. In other words, the color sequence is A, B, B, A, B, B, A.....and so on.

First stitch, white, second stitch, black, third stitch, black:

Fourth stitch, white. fifth stitch, black, sixth stitch, black:

This gives a plaited look, as if the white stitches were actually being woven over and under the black stitches.

Herringbone Color Series II

Another color alternation pattern works <u>against</u> the three-repeat structure to create a line of alternating dark and light X's. Do the first two stitches in Color A, the next two in Color B, and so forth. In other words, the color sequence is A, A, B, B, A, A, B, B....and so on.

Can you see the alternating X's beginning to emerge?

Herringbone Three-Color Series

Choose three colors and work in sequence. For the example diagrams we'll use white, grey and black.

First stitch white, second stitch grey, third stitch, black:

Repeat white, grey, black for the fourth, fifth and sixth stitches.

Notice how as you begin each new stitch, you use the same color beads as the stitch that ended at that point. (Look at the arrows!)

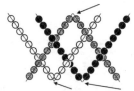

This fools the eye into thinking that it's actually seeing 3 continuous lines of beads:

white, grey, and black

cleverly braided together into a single sumptuous strand.

CHAPTER FOURTEEN: LOOP STITCH

This works best with the BCB technique; anything else loses the characteristic raised loop in the middle of the stitch.

It is very helpful to draw parallel lines as guidelines for working this stitch. I find that for lines about 3/8" to ½" apart I need about 10 seed beads for the initial stitch and about 25-26 for each stitch thereafter.

Bring needle up at A, string on 10 seed beads and bring needle down at B; this shouldn't be the full length of the 10 seed bead string but should allow them to droop in a gentle curve as shown in the diagram.

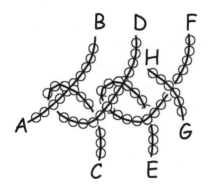

Bring needle up at C, directly below B. String on 26 seed beads; slide them down against the fabric and hold them relatively taut, with no thread showing, while you loop the string of beads first over the previous stitch, then under it, then over itself and bring the needle down again at D, at the top of the two guidelines. Just try it; this is harder to explain than it is to do!

Bring the needle up again at E, string on 26 beads, pass the strung beads under the previous stitch, then over it, then under itself, and bring needle down at F on the top guideline.

When you are ready to stop making loops, close the stitch by bringing the needle up between the guide lines, as shown at G, and stringing on 4 to 8 seed beads to cross over and anchor the last stitch by going down at H.

[Tip: if you have trouble maintaining the tension, so that your beads from the previous stitch tend to open up and make space for a TCT crossing instead of the BCB that you want, take a tiny back stitch at the beginning of each new stitch to hold the previous one in place.]

Sequin or Decorative Bead Loop Stitch

Bring needle up at A, string (10 sb, sequin) and bring needle down at B

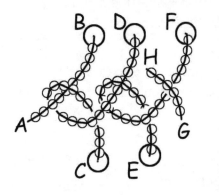

Bring needle up at C, directly below B. String on (sequin, 26 sb, sequin). Loop this string of beads first over the previous stitch, then under it, then over itself and bring the needle down again at D, at the top of the two guidelines.

Continue making loops as for the basic stitch, stringing (sequin, 26 sb, sequin) each time until you are ready to end the line of stitching; then finish with an anchor stitch of 4 to 6 beads, as for the basic stitch. Instead of a sequin you can use a small decorative bead (E bead, Miyuki cube or triangle, 3-4 mm crystal, small pearl, etc.) Depending on the size of the bead and the sharpness of the edges, you may want to buffer the decorative bead with a seed bead after it.

Bugle Bead Loop Stitch

I'm not going to repeat the detailed instructions for bugle beads; they are almost exactly the same as for sequins. For your first stitch from A to B, string (7 sb, bb, sb). For subsequent stitches, string (sb, bb, 22 sb, bb, sb)

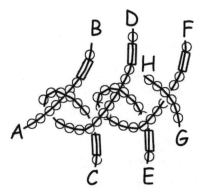

[Note: as if I hadn't said this often enough already: the numbers of seed beads given are just suggestions. You may find that using a few seed beads more or less fits your stitching style better. For this particular stitch, I do strongly suggest that you allow at least 12 seed beads between the bugles, or your loops of beads will be tight and difficult to work.]

Dangles

Another easy variation is to add a dangle to the bottom edge of the stitch.

Begin as for basic loop stitch: Bring needle up at A, string on 10 seed beads and bring needle down at B.

Bring needle up at C, directly below B. Take a **very tiny** backstitch to stabilize the beads.

Now thread on your dangle beads: in the diagram, I've chosen a dangle of (8 sb, crystal, sb). Using the last seed bead as a pivot, pass back through the crystal and the 8 seed beads. Now thread on 26 seed 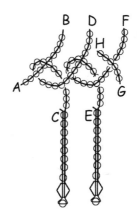 beads, loop under and around the curve AB as usual, and bring needle down at D.

Repeat this sequence of backstitch, dangle, and loop until you are ready to end the line of stitching with a short anchor stitch as usual.

Double Dangles

If you're working this stitch vertically rather than horizontally, you may want to add a dangle on each side, letting them hang down to create a rich internal fringe.

CHAPTER FIFTEEN: ROSE STITCHES

These two stitches aren't actually structurally related, but their purpose is the same: to make detached rose-like motifs.

Straight Stitch Rose

This isn't so much a new stitch as just a way of working straight, or satin, or lazy stitch – just four or five beads on a string – around a center. It's popular in silk ribbon embroidery as one of the many ways to make a vaguely rose-shaped form, and it works just as well in bead embroidery; the beads, rather than the width of the ribbon, give dimension to the piece.

Start with a largeish decorative bead in the center; an E bead, a big triangle bead, a 4mm crystal or a small pearl all work well; if you want to use something even bigger as your center, you'll need to work a really big rose around it to keep things in proportion.

Once the center bead is stitched down, bring the needle up close beside it at A, thread on 3 to 5 beads, and come down again close to the bead at B. It's best if you make the stitch a little shorter than the length measured by the beads, so that you get a gentle loop rather than a strained, taut line.

Backstitch and bring the needle up at C outside your first loop, but still close to the center bead. Thread on at least as many beads as you used the previous time and make another straight stitch, going a little farther around the central bead and coming down at D.

It's almost impossible to show this clearly in a two-dimensional diagram. Do you see how the beads for this second stitch cover up the letter B marking the insertion point for the first stitch? I'm showing the beads as if they were lying flat against the base fabric. Actually each stitch will force the previous loop up a little bit, so that the effect you get is of slightly raised petals clustered around a center, with little or no background fabric showing.

For the third stitch, come up at E, just outside the loop of the second stitch but still as close as possible to the center bead. String on as many beads as you need to make a graceful loop around to come down at A; you'll want more than five this time because your stitch has to go around some of the beads of the second stitch.

[Note: the instruction to "come down at A" is based on the assumption that you're using a triangular bead as your center. If you have a square bead you probably won't return to your starting point until the fourth stitch; if you have a large or oddly shaped bead, it may take five or more stitches to work all the way around it.]

Repeat this pattern of coming up just outside the previous stitch, making a loop around the next corner, and coming down just outside the existing beads again....

…and again and again and again, until the rose shape is as big as you want it. After a few stitches you'll probably find that you need 12 or more beads to make a loop from the center of one existing stitch to the center of the next existing stitch. When the shape gets that large, I usually start just making short little 8-bead loops, continuing to bury the beginning and the end of each stitch under the existing loops, so that I don't have a long unanchored stitch of 15 or more beads flapping loosely at the edge of the shape.

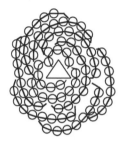

In the pictured example I've added some loops of blue-green beads, for leaves, under the basic rose form.

Spiderweb Rose

To make the woven (or pseudo-woven) look of the spiderweb stitch, you need to start with an odd number of lines. Seven is good; nine is generally too many, five too sparse, and three way too sparse. (Traditional embroidery uses five, but embroidery thread packs down closer than beads do; I find that with only five spokes the lines of beads between spokes get way too long.)

Drawing seven evenly spaced lines radiating from a center point is not easy. If you like fooling around with a protractor, you've probably figured out that adjacent lines have to be at approximately a 51 $\frac{1}{2}$ degree angle apart, and you can sit there with your protractor and mark out the angles precisely.

If, like me, you can't remember where the last kid to take geometry left the protractor, you can think of the angle as "a tad more than 45 degrees" and draw by what engineers call "the eyeball algorithm." If you take this approach, I recommend you practice for a while on scrap paper before marking up your fabric!

Or you can always copy this diagram and trace it onto your fabric.

Now you want to lay down lines of back stitch following the diagram, with the same

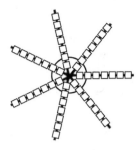

number of beads in each line. I like to use Delicas for this; they're neat and even and easy to "weave" over and under in the next step. I also like to put a sequin right in the center, so that when I start "weaving" I don't have to squish the beads right down to the middle where the lines of Delicas come together. This sequin will hardly be visible when the weaving is complete. It's kind of a "security sequin", to make absolutely sure the background fabric doesn't show through where you don't want it to, rather than a decoration in its own right.

Once the lines of backstitched beads are laid down, I like to start a new thread in the color of the beads I'm going to weave through. Bring this thread up at A - at the edge of the sequin, right beside one of the beaded spokes. String on enough of your weaving beads to go around the edge of the sequin, over the next spoke, and down to the very edge of the next spoke. (Obviously exact numbers will depend on the size of your sequin and the size of your beads. I usually start with 3 to 5 beads and increase by a bead or two every time I go around the circle.)

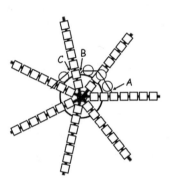

Take a tiny stitch at B, right underneath this spoke, bring the needle back up at C, just barely on the far side of the spoke.

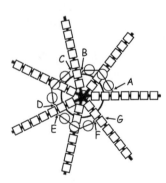

Repeat, coming down at D and up at E, down at F and up at G.

Now you've almost completed the circle. Notice that in this next round you are stitching <u>over</u> the spoke where you started weaving and are about to go <u>under</u> the first spoke you passed over in the beginning. This is why you wanted an odd number of spokes.

For the next stitch, coming up at G, string on as many beads as it takes to go over the next spoke and the beads of the previous stitch and bring the needle down at H. If you look closely at the diagram, you'll see that while I was using 3 beads per stitch up to now, this stitch requires 5 beads – two more than before.

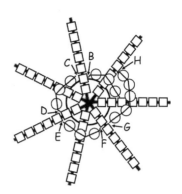

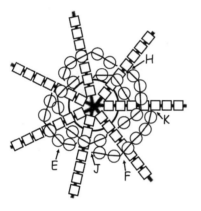

Continue around the circle with these longer stitches until you have almost completed the circle again. When you bring your needle up at J (far side of the spoke between E and F in the previous diagram) your next stitch will have to cover slightly more territory before you can come down at K, because you're going to go around the first couple of beads in the stitch between G and H (see previous diagram) and you'll have to allow for the way they angle up to go around the very first stitch you took.

Continue in this manner, "weaving" over alternate spikes and increasing the number of beads per stitch as needed, until all the spikes are covered.

Depending on the length of your spokes, you may find as you approach the outer edge of the form that you're needing more beads than you're comfortable with to go from one spoke, over the next, and down at the next. Once I get to having more than 11 or 12 beads to a stitch, I generally forget about the woven structure – which is getting

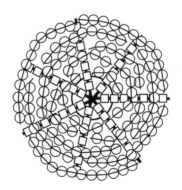

kind of diffuse at this point anyway – and finish the form off with loops of 6 to 11 beads packed tightly around the outside to cover the last vestiges of the spoke stitches.

Look at the color pictures to see some of the effects you can get by changing bead colors as you work around the spiderweb.

CHAPTER SIXTEEN: SATIN STITCH

If you've done bead embroidery, you probably know this as "lazy stitch." I've always hated this name, because there's nothing lazy about beading, so I refuse to use it. Anyway, it's exactly a beadwork analog to the embroiderers' satin stitch.

Instead of making a long line of beads and continually stitching back through the previous beads as with back stitch, you just do short lines – needle up, string on four to six beads, needle down. What could be simpler? What could be more open to interesting variations?

Shaded Line Satin Stitch

Stitch overlapping lines of seed beads in a color or light/dark gradated pattern and make a broad curving line.

Bugle Bead Broad Line Satin Stitch

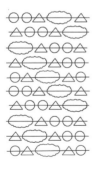

Make a thick line with stitches composed of a seed bead-bugle bead-seed bead sequence. (This is a good way to use bugle beads in any case; the seed beads on either end buffer the thread so it doesn't fray against the sharp ends of the bugle beads.)

Textured Satin Stitch

Build up texture with overlapping satin stitches using beads in a small/medium/large sequence (for instance: 11/0 seed bead, 8/0 triangle, freshwater pearl, 8/0 triangle, 11/0 seed bead).

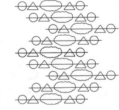

One way to keep the lines close together is to stagger the stitches so that you're never trying to put two large central beads next to each other.

Another is to cycle through the sequence of beads, starting each stitch with the next one up – i.e., in the sequence (sb, tri, prl, tri, sb) suggested above, your first 5 stitches would actually be as follows:

Stitch 1: (sb, tri, prl, tri, sb)
Stitch 2: (tri, prl, tri, sb, sb)
Stitch 3: (prl, tri, sb, sb, tri)
Stitch 4: (tri, sb, sb, tri, prl)
Stitch 5: (sb, sb, tri, prl, tri)

Shaped Satin Stitch Filling

Small shapes can be completely filled in by short lines of satin stitch.

Of course, there's no legal requirement that you make all the beads the same color, or even the same type; you can border the shape with a contrasting color and put bugles in the middle if you like.

You can accent a part of the shape with larger beads, preferably beads twice as high as the seed beads around them, so that two lines of seed beads go through each accent bead, as here:

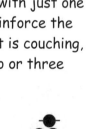

Tip: If you look at the pictured examples, you'll notice that some of the "satin stitch" lines have as many as 18 or 20 beads. That's a lot to hold down with just one straight stitch, so when my lines start getting too long, I begin to reinforce the satin stitch by working back through them. One simple reinforcement is couching, but I find I usually get a smoother line by stitching back through two or three beads in the line wherever it needs holding down.

Shaded Satin Stitch Filling

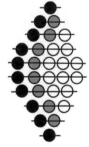

With beaded satin stitch it's easy to shade a filled area; all you do is pick up beads in progressively darker shades of the color you're working in, so each individual stitch can be shaded. (If you were embroidering in thread, you would have to keep changing threads and work back into the filling with new stitches for each color.)

Basket Weave Satin Stitch

By working rows of beads in different directions you can create various kinds of basket weave effects with satin stitch. The effect is strongest if the contrast between different directions is strongest, so it's a good place to juxtapose rows of bugle beads with rows of seed beads. If you're using beads of the same shape and color in both directions, remember that shiny, light colored beads will reflect the way light and shadow change with the direction of the stitch and will show off the contrasts more effectively than matte finish, dark colored beads. If you're counting on color contrast to show the pattern, bear in mind that from a distance, value stands out more than color, and choose a light value of one color and a dark value of the other.

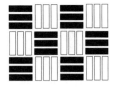 Using contrasting colors of bugle beads produces a strong patterned effect. If you try this, though, look for bugle beads with smooth ends so that your thread won't be cut by the sharp edges typical of bugles.

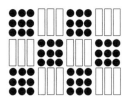

Working with contrasting colors of bugles and seed beads can add textural impact.

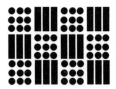 Using similar colors of bugles and seed beads gives a textured-only effect, very subtle.

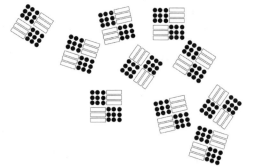

This stitch is also effective for making small square motifs to be scattered over an interesting background.

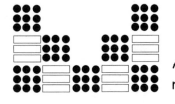

And, of course, you don't have to stay in the strictly rectangular format; play with shapes to fit your design.

CHAPTER SEVENTEEN: VANDYKE STITCH

Like loop stitch, this really needs to be worked in BCB style to get the plaited effect in the middle of the stitch. This stitch also is worked between two parallel lines, but I find it easier to work down (guidelines vertical) than from one side to the other (guidelines horizontal). As always, the number of beads you need is approximate; I find that to fill a space $\frac{3}{4}$" wide I need at least ten seed beads for the two starting stitches and twenty to thirty thereafter.

Basic Vandyke Stitch

It's helpful to draw two faint parallel lines about $\frac{3}{4}$" apart as guides for this stitch. You may also want to draw a center line just at the beginning, to guide your initial stitch placement; you won't need it after that.

Bring needle up at A on the lefthand line, string on 10 seed beads, and bring down at B – just to the right of the center line, forming a graceful, gentle curve. (If the beads are stretched taut in a straight line, you don't have enough of them; add one or two at a time until you get a curve that looks like the diagram.)

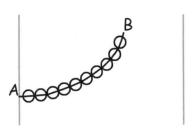

In a moment you're going to be passing a line of seed beads *under* this curve, so you want to be sure and leave enough room for that.

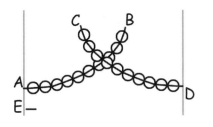

For the next stitch you'll need slightly more beads, because your line of seed beads in this stitch is going to cross over the curving line you just made. If you used 10 seed beads in the first stitch, use 12 now. Come up beside B at C – just to the left of the center - string on your seed beads and bring needle down at D, parallel to A and right on the righthand guide line.

Bring needle up at E, ready to start the third stitch. This time, instead of bringing the needle down in the middle, you will string on enough seed beads to go all the way across with a loop in the middle – twenty-five to thirty, probably. I would suggest you start with twenty, make the loop as described below, and check to see if you have enough beads to bring the needle down comfortably. If not, add on one or two at a time until the length of strung beads is sufficient.

Once the beads are strung on, pass the needle and the string of beads under the beads between C and D below the point where they cross with the curve AB, bring it up over the short ends near C and B, and go back under the curve AB below the cross.

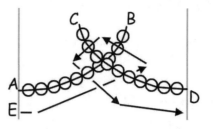

This is the path you follow.

I would recommend that you lightly pinch the beading thread between thumb and forefinger now and slide your hand down until you are touching the strung beads and holding them taut to the cloth, to make sure that the string of beads hasn't separated anywhere under the loop and given you a TCT crossing. Once you're sure of that, and if you have enough beads on the string to reach the righthand guide line easily, you can bring the needle down at F, exactly opposite E. Your beads should look like this:

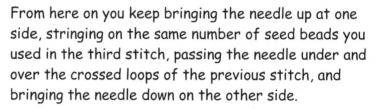

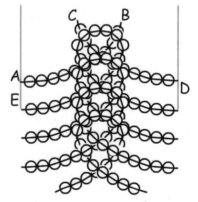

From here on you keep bringing the needle up at one side, stringing on the same number of seed beads you used in the third stitch, passing the needle under and over the crossed loops of the previous stitch, and bringing the needle down on the other side.

No special finishing stitch is necessary; just tie off the thread when you have worked the desired length.

If you'd like to bring the stitch to a neat point at the ending, you can do it as follows:

Bring the needle up halfway between the lefthand guide line and the center. String on fewer beads than you have been using – if you were stringing 24 beads for each stitch, try 18 this time, and increase or decrease as necessary to loop around the previous stitch and come down halfway between the center and the righthand guide line.

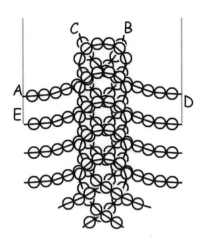

Now bring the needle up just to the left of the center line. String on just enough beads to loop around the previous stitch and come down just to the right of the center line.

You can see examples of this tapering close in the color pictures for the dangle and sequin variations, below, and on the beaded mermaid necklace in Chapter 18.

Close Vandyke Stitch

In traditional embroidery the loop of the Vandyke stitch is not nearly so prominent, so you seldom see this variation. But in bead embroidery, where the central portion of the stitch is so prominently raised, you may want to work the stitch so that only the loop portion really shows. For this, try putting your guidelines 3/8" apart, instead of $\frac{3}{4}$". Work the first stitch with 6 seed beads, the second with 8, the third and subsequent ones with 18 to 20.

In the color picture example I've started and ended with two stitches of pink seed beads, while for the body of the work I've alternated pink and blue seed bead stitches to emphasize the braided effect.

Vandyke Stitch with Bugle Beads

Bring needle up at A, string (sb, bugle, 6 sb) and bring down at B.

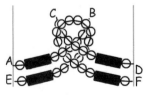

Bring needle up at C, string (sb, bugle, 8 sb), cross over loop AB and bring needle down at D.

Bring needle up at E and string (sb, bb, 20 sb, bb, sb). Holding the beads in place so that they don't slide apart and allow a thread crossing instead of a bead crossing, bring needle and beads under CD below the X where CD crosses AB, across and over both AB and CD above the crossing, and under AB. Bring needle down at F.

String all subsequent stitches with the sequence (sb, bugle, 20 sb, bugle, sb).

[Note: the actual number of seed beads you need in the middle of the stitch depends on several variables: the width of the space you're trying to cover, the length and diameter of your beads, even how well they do or don't nest together. 20 is just my best estimate. Count beads and make your own estimate to suit your style.)

All subsequent stitches follow the pattern of loop EF.

Vandyke Stitch with Sequins or Decorative Beads

This works almost exactly like the bugle bead variation.

Bring needle up at A, thread on (sequin, 10 sb) and bring down at B.

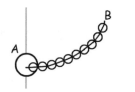

Bring needle up at C, thread on (sequin, 11 sb) and bring down at D.

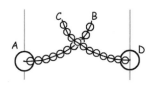

Bring needle up at E, thread on (sequin, 26 sb, sequin) and follow the usual twisty path – under CD below the crossing point, around and over AB and CD above their crossing point, under AB below the crossing point, and finally down at F.

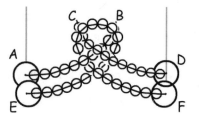

All subsequent stitches follow the pattern of EF.

Instead of a sequin you can use a small decorative bead (E bead, Miyuki cube or triangle, 3-4 mm crystal, small pearl, etc.) Depending on the size of the bead and the sharpness of the edges, you may want to buffer the decorative bead with a seed bead after it.

Vandyke Stitch with Dangles

Bring needle up at A as usual, but instead of threading on the loop beads immediately, first thread on your dangle sequence – in these diagrams, the sequence is (9sb, cube, sb). Using the last seed bead as a pivot, go back through the cube and the first nine seed beads and draw the thread reasonably tight (you want the dangle to rest against the fabric without any unsightly stretches of bare thread, but you don't want to pull it so tightly that it pops out and tries to stand out perpendicular to the fabric.) *Now* thread (10 sb) and bring needle down at B.

If maintaining the desired tension is a problem, consider taking a very tiny backstrich after you come back up through the dangle seed beads, but before you start the loop from A to B:

The next stitch, from C to D, will be almost the reverse of stitch AB.

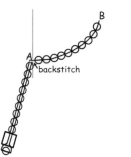

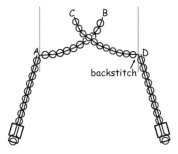

Bring the needle up at C and thread on (20 sb, cube, sb). Using the last seed bead as a pivot, pass back through the cube and the nine seed beads of the dangle; then bring the needle down at D. Again, it may help to maintain tension if you take a small backstitch at D, after threading the 11 loop beads and before starting the dangle.

Now for the long, complicated stitch. Try not to hold your breath while performing the following sequence of operations:

Bring needle up at E.

String on (9sb, cube, sb) and go back through the cube and the nine seed beads of the dangle.

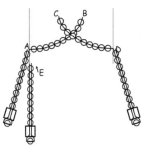

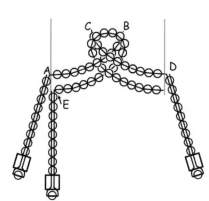

String the 26 (or however many you're using) seed beads for the basic stitch, then bring that line of seed beads up, under the curve CD below the crossing point, over both CD and AB above the point where they cross, and down under the curve AB below the cross. And don't bring that needle down yet!

You still need to string on the dangle beads at the end of the stitch. Go on, breathe, then string (9sb, cube, sb), go back through the cube and the 9 seed beads, and then bring the needle down at F.

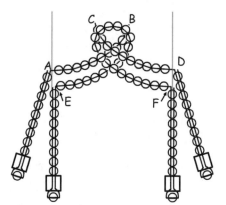

In the color picture example I've worked several stitches of basic Vandyke before beginning to add the dangles.

CHAPTER EIGHTEEN: PROJECTS AND EXAMPLES

Pocket Doll

This little doll can be made out of any scrap of fabric you have on hand. She's small enough to bead in an evening and a convenient size to carry in your pocket, or you can prop her on a bookshelf or bead a cord to turn her into a pendant.

The pattern was sketched from drawings in Marija Gimbutas' <u>The Goddesses and Gods of Old Europe</u>; the originals of the drawings were bone figurines found in Bulgaria, dating from 4000-4500 BC.

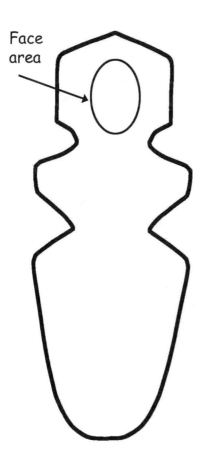

Face area

You can scan and enlarge this pattern to any size you're comfortable with, or have a copy shop do it for you. I wouldn't suggest making it any smaller as very small pieces are difficult to turn and stuff.

Note: If you plan to use a bead or cabochon for the face, I'd recommend tracing around the cabochon and enlarging the pattern until it fits comfortably within the head area like the oval in the pattern. Otherwise you're liable to wind up with a "face" that's too big or too small in proportion to the doll.

With such a small, simple pattern I don't bother tracing it onto the fabric; I just cut the shape out of copy paper, pin it to the fabric, and stitch around it, leaving an opening for turning and stuffing, like this.

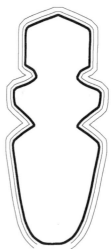

I like to use a shorter stitch length than normal and to sew a double seam; stuffing the doll firmly puts a lot of pressure on the seam, and making a strong double seam to begin with is a lot less trouble than mending places where the stuffing pops out later.

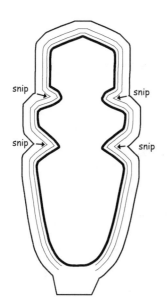

After the seams are sewn, cut out very close to the outer seam, leaving a bit of extra fabric at the opening where you will turn and stuff. Snip the inside curves right down to within one or two threads of the outer seam (at the places indicated by arrows).

Now turn the doll inside out and stuff her through the opening with polyester stuffing or scraps of quilt batting. To avoid lumps, it's better to use lots of tiny scraps than a few big pieces. Make sure that the head and arms are fully stuffed before you stuff the lower body.

Two tools are very useful at this point. A hemostat allows you to reach inside the stitched form, grab the seam at the top of the head and pull, which makes it easy to turn a small piece inside out. A stuffing fork will hold small pieces of stuffing while you push them into the crevices of the figure. Neither is absolutely necessary, though; your fingers and a chopstick will do the job, it'll just be a bit more work.

When the body is fully stuffed, turn the fabric at the opening under and whipstitch it closed.

If you're going to use a face cab, now is the time to glue it on. Try it on the stuffed form first and make sure you're happy with it. I had picked out a perfectly good copper face bead for this doll, but at this point she informed me that she didn't want that bead or any other realistic face; she wanted a plain oval mother of pearl cabochon. You have to listen to the work as you go along; it'll tell you what it wants. I attached the cabochon with a dab of Aleene's Tacky Glue and let it dry overnight.

General information about beading a stuffed form

Beginning a thread:
 Tie a single knot in the end of your thread. Insert the needle some distance away from where you want to come out, bring it out where you want to start beading, and gently tug the thread until the knot pops through the outer fabric. You want that knot to stay buried in the stuffing, so don't pull so hard that it comes right out the other side!

Ending a thread:
Bring the needle out close to some beads you've already stitched on, or in an area that you know will be covered with beads later. Take a very tiny backstitch, then tie

a knot in the thread about ¼ to ½ inch from the fabric. Insert the needle for a good long distance (in the case of a doll as small as this one, you might just go right through the body) and, again, gently tug on the thread until your knot pops through to the stuffing.

Getting the needle to come up where you want it:

This isn't always as simple as when you're embroidering on a flat surface, especially when you have a tightly stuffed object with lots of curves. A lot of times you won't be able to work the stitch exactly as described in the diagrams; you'll have to take an intermediate stitch, hopefully into some area where the thread will be covered with beads, and then stitch back to where you want the needle to come up. I'll describe this in more detail when we get to the rows of bugle bead fly stitch below.

Beading around a cabochon

If you already know how to bead around a cabochon with peyote stitch, skip this and go to the next section, "Back to bead embroidery".

Once the glue is dry, I like to make a cabochon really secure by beading around it and just over its edge with peyote stitch. That's not strictly bead embroidery, since we'll be building a structure with beads upon beads rather than just beads on cloth, but we might as well go over it.

You start by working a row of seed beads around the cabochon in good old simple backstitch, so that it looks like this from above

and like this from the side:

Ok, we all know there's a thread running through those beads to hold them to the cloth, but we're not going to worry about that thread any more; that was just the backstitch, and you know how to do that.

Now you're going to bring the needle up between two of those beads you just stitched down, pass through one bead, string on one bead, skip the next bead in the original backstitched line, and pass the needle through the third bead in that line, like this:

Keep on going that way around the entire original oval until you're back at your starting point, so that any side view of the  beads looks like this:

What you do next depends on whether you had an odd or even number of beads in the original backstitched oval. It doesn't make any difference in the long run; it just determines how you make the next step up.

If you had an odd number of beads, as in the diagram above, then you're going to finish the oval in this configuration:
 and your next step will be to bring the thread up, thread on one bead and pass through the first bead of the second layer, leaving a one-bead gap behind you which will be filled in when you complete the circle again.

If you had an even number of beads originally, then you're going to finish the oval in this configuration: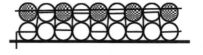

Your next step is the same as in the previous case – you thread on one new bead and pass through the first bead of the second layer – but in this case you don't have to bring the thread up, and you won't be leaving a gap behind you.

In either case, now you work round the row of sticking-up beads you created in the first pass, threading on a new bead and passing through an old bead, until all the gaps in the oval are filled. In this diagram I've shaded the beads of the third pass to show the pattern of alternation more clearly; in fact of course you'll be using beads of the same color throughout, unless you want a speckled effect.

Note that it takes two passes of peyote stitch to put on as many beads as you did in the first layer of backstitch.

With a doll as small as this one, you're probably using a small thin cabochon, so two passes of peyote stitch should be enough to frame it. If you pull the thread taut the beads will curve in just a little, following the curve of the cabochon, and help to hold it in place.

For absolute security, or if you're using a big thick cabochon, add another two passes of peyote stitch to make a frame three beads high. Work the third pass exactly like the first two, adding on every other bead, but do the fourth pass slightly differently: occasionally skip adding a bead and go straight through two successive beads of the third pass, like this:

I know, I know, in the picture it looks as if that'll create an awful gap, but when you try it in three dimensions you'll see that it works. Cabochons normally have a domed top so that their side profile looks like this; you can see that the higher layers of beads have to go around a shorter distance than the bottom layer. There's no hard and fast rule for how often to skip a bead in this fourth peyote pass; it depends on the size and slope of your cabochon. Look at the beads on the third layer, and when it seems that two of them are leaning together and could be drawn close to each other with a pull on the thread, that's when you skip a bead.

Whew! I'm glad that's over; it took a <u>lot</u> longer to explain than to do! There are lots of exciting and creative things you can do with peyote stitch, but this isn't one of them. It's extremely useful, though.

Back to bead embroidery

Now that the "face" is on and securely attached, let's begin embroidering at the bottom of the doll and work up. Begin by working a series of overlapping dangle stitches for a "skirt", to create a rich fringe that just allows the base fabric to show through.

The first round of stitching is a buttonhole dangle in SBT style. The stem part of the buttonhole is 4 lavender seed beads and the dangle part is 6 lavender seed beads, 1 green bugle bead, 1 seed bead, 1 lavender baroque pearl, and 1 seed bead for the pivot; so the stringing sequence for each stitch is (10 sb, bb, sb, pearl, sb) and you string back through (pearl, sb, bb, 6 sb).

For the next round, repeat this stitch, offsetting it slightly so that the dangles fall

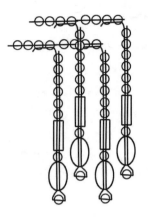

halfway between the dangles of the first round. Because the doll body tapers, this round has to cover slightly more territory than the first round. Occasionally you will need 5 seed beads instead of 4 for the stem part, so that the stringing sequence becomes (11 sb, bb, sb, pearl, sb). You still string back through (pearl, sb, bb, 6 sb).

For the third and fourth rounds stay with the lavender seed beads, green bugles, and lavender pearls in a buttonhole SBT dangle, but add a little to the dangle. The stem is still (4 sb) or (5 sb) but the dangle part of the sequence is now (3sb, bb, sb, bb, sb, pearl, sb).

After four rounds of fringed buttonhole stitch there should be a nice deep fringe covering the bottom of the dall.

Switch to fly stitch, working TCT style with the loop composed of matte blue seed beads and twisted silver-lined bugles. *Read the instructions all the way through before you start stitching; to work on a small 3D form you're going to have to learn some new tricks.*

In the first round the stringing sequence is (sb, bb, 2sb, bb, sb), the loop points up, and there are no beads on the anchor stitch.

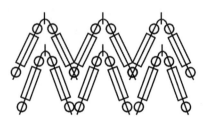

For the second round you want to start the loop stitches deep in the V's formed by the previous round. This means that they begin where there isn't much space between the bugle beads of the first round, so you need to make them share a bead at the end as shown in the diagram. The first loop of the round is strung with a seed bead at both ends (sb, bb, 2sb, bb, sb), subsequent loops are strung using the last seed bead of the previous loop as their starting point (sb, bb, 2sb, bb), and the very last loop uses previously strung seed beads at both beginning and end (bb, 2sb, bb).

This fly stitch series is difficult to work in the normal way on a rounded figure. Each figure will dictate its own "rules" as you adapt stitches to the space available and to the curves you have to conform to. In this case I found it was easier to work the fly stitch loops in sequence, stitching each one after the first <u>backwards</u>, and then to go back and put in the anchor stitches. So the formation of the initial round went like this:

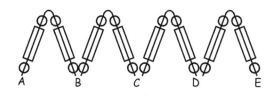

Needle up at A, string (sb, bb, 2sb, bb, sb), down at B. So far we're doing the same thing as for basic fly stitch. But it would be difficult to bring the needle from B to the top of the stitch to form the anchor; because of the way the doll figure is curved here, it's much easier to bring the needle up at C. String (sb, bb, 2sb, bb, sb) and bring the needle <u>back</u> to B – you're actually forming the loop backwards, but don't worry; it looks exactly the same.

Now you can push the needle from B to D before it comes out, make another backwards loop stitch ending at C, then go through the doll form from C to E, and so on. When the round is finished, you go back and tack down each loop stitch with a tiny anchor stitch between the two top seed beads.

The third round of fly stitch comes close to the waist of the doll, so you can use it to give her a girdle of purple sequins. Each stitch in this row is anchored not with a single tiny stitch of thread but with 2 seed beads and a sequin. The doll image here is not quite accurate; actually the sequins will overlap, as you can see in the color picture.

Above the sequins, decorate her torso with a winding line of green seed beads in backstitch. When the line is finished, interlace it on alternating sides (see Threaded Backstitch, in chapter 3). Each interlacing stitch consists of 2 lavender seed beads, one blue triangle bead, and 2 lavender seed beads.

Cover the rest of the doll's torso with matte transparent green beads in satin stitch.

Now for the head. It would be nice to make her "hair" refer to some of the other beadwork, so try working a backstitch around the existing beadwork with the lavender seed beads, every so often inserting a dangle that uses the same green bugles and lavender baroque pearls that were used in the first three rows of buttonhole stitch with dangles. After a few rows of this backstitch with dangles you can finish covering the top and back of the head with simple dangles.

Mermaid Necklace

For this piece you will need 2 pieces of Ultrasuede about 5" x 8" and a small oval cabochon or flattish oval bead. If you decide to use the foiling method described below, you will also need a piece of Wonder Under, a piece of plastic-backed foil, and parchment paper, all 5"x8". It's not necessary to foil the Ultrasuede but I like to do so, since in one step it gives you a wonderful shimmery background and marks your pattern. See Suppliers list in back of book if you don't know where to find the foil.

Foiling will give you a finished piece that is the mirror image of the pattern provided here. That shouldn't be a problem in this case, unless you really care strongly about which way your mermaid's tail curves; if it's important to you, scan the pattern and flip it horizontally, or trace it on tracing paper with a strong black marker and turn it over.

Transferring the pattern

If foiling: Lay your piece of Wonder Under over the pattern and trace it. Cut out the Wonder Under *exactly* along the pattern lines, being careful not to let the fusible web separate from the paper. Lay it down on one of your Ultrasuede pieces, paper side up; cover with parchment paper and press lightly for 3-5 seconds. Let the Ultrasuede and Wonder Under cool slightly, then gently peel away the paper, leaving a fusible-web mermaid shape on the Ultrasuede. Lay the plastic-backed foil over this, *colored side up* (this is counterintuitive if you're not used to foiling; pay attention!), cover with parchment paper and just make one or two quick swoops across the paper with a hot iron. Lift the parchment paper and gently peel away the foil. You should be left with a foiled mermaid shape on the Ultrasuede. (If not all the foil stuck the first time around, you can try laying a new piece over the figure and foiling again; sometimes you get wonderful color mixes this way.)

If you choose not to foil, but to let the Ultrasuede itself be the background: copy the pattern, cut it out and draw lightly around the shape with pencil. This will be your cutting line when the time comes to trim the piece, so be sure never to sew right into the pencil line while you are beading.

Face Cabochon

Like the Pocket Doll, this piece is so small that a simple flat bead or small cabochon works well for a "face." I used a vintage flat-backed glass leaf shape, held on first with glue and then with a beaded bezel. A flat bead can be sewn on; to attach and bead around a cabochon, see the directions for the Pocket Doll project.

Beading the Tail

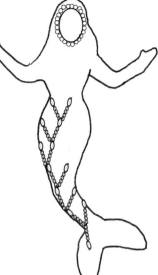

Once the face cabochon is attached, I like to start the mermaid with the lower part of the body. No particular reason; you've got to start somewhere. Beginning at the waist, work a lopsided feather stitch all the way down the side of her body, branching out towards the edge as often as necessary rather than alternating stitches regularly. I used dark green pearls to accent the ends of the feather stitch and a combination of iridescent green Delica seed

beads and darker green bugle beads for the body of the stitch. If you're not used to working feather stitch to fit into an irregular space, I'd recommend you skip the bugle beads and just work with seed beads; that gives you a little more flexibility. The last feather stitch ends with a long anchor stitch reaching down into the fin area.

Start again, back up at the waist, and bead along the right side of the figure the same way, again ending with an anchor stitch that reaches out into the fins.

Finally, work whatever additional feather stitches you need to fill in the middle, and fill in the fins with lines of backstitch fanning out from the anchor stitches and using the same mix of beads and pearls. (If you look at the color picture of the mermaid you'll see that there are more stitches actually worked than I could show on this drawing. It's a *simplified* diagram, ok?)

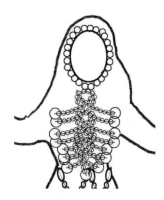

Beading the Torso

We've got a sort of tapered rectangular area here just begging to be filled with something textured and flashy; a perfect place for Vandyke stitch. I used silver-lined pink seed beads and small pink Swarovski crystals with an AB finish. The stitch begins at the neck and tapers down to a point at the waist, merging with the feather stitching of the tail.

Beading the Arms

Not all the beadwork has to be fancy stitching. Fill in the arms with close-stitched rows of plain backstitch; I used the same silver-lined pink seed beads that I used for the torso, but a different color – perhaps the same beads used for the tail – would work equally well. Bead well up into the area around the head.

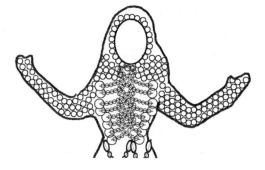

Beading around the Face

Work this section as for the Pocket Doll, beading around the face with backstitch and dangles. I used the same iridescent green delicas that were used in the tail beadwork, with dangles combining delicas, bugles and pearls in the sequence (2sb, bb, 2sb, bb, 2sb, bb, 2sb, bb, 2sb, pearl, sb).

Edge and Fringes

Before edging, glue the beaded ultrasuede piece to the other, unmarked piece. When the glue is dry, trim both layers along the edge marked by foil or pencil, being careful not to cut any threads.

I've got three basic approaches to edging these suede-based bead embroideries:

(1) Who needs an edging? It looks just fine as it is.

(2) A beaded edge would be neater and would also catch those places where I didn't quite glue the two pieces of suede together perfectly, but I don't want a big clunky edge, so I'll do a modified brick stitch.

(3) This sucker is going to know it's got an edge; I'm going to whipstitch seed beads all the way around.

For the mermaid I used approach (2), which means that now you get to do a little brick stitch. If you're familiar with off-loom beadwork this will be easy. If you aren't, don't worry, it'll still be easy.

Your thread will show with this stitch, so you want to pick a thread that's as close as possible to the color of your edging beads. For the mermaid's head and tail, I used the same iridescent green Delicas and turquoise thread I had used for the tail embroidery.

Begin stitching the tail edging at the top of the green beadwork: start by pushing your needle in at the back and between the layers of Ultrasuede so that it comes out where you want to start the edging. Let a little tail of thread show on the back; you can hold this with your thumb while you secure the thread with a tiny backstitch, then pull it the loose tail taut and clip it off.

Start by stringing on two seed beads, then bring the needle down and pass from the *back* of the edge to the *front* of the edge. Here's how it looks if you lay the mermaid down flat and squint at the edge (the thick dark line is the Ultrasuede) .

Now, with your needle coming out the *front* side of the edge, go back through the bead you just stitched on, entering the bead from the bottom (side nearest the Ultrasuede) and exiting from the top.

String on another bead, bring the needle down and pass from back to front and back through the new bead.

As you keep working this way, your thread will do two jobs at once for you: it will hold the beads in a nice even line along the outside edge of the piece, and it will hold the two pieces of Ultrasuede together (just in case you missed a spot with the glue).

As you work your way down towards the fins, you're going to want to start adding a dangle to each edge stitch. Remember that the mermaid's tail is curved, it doesn't hang straight down, so you don't just start the dangles at the same point on each side; you need to hold her up by the arms, the way she's going to hang, and decide where the dangles should start. The line across the bottom here shows approximately where you'll want to start the tail dangles.

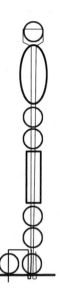

To add a dangle: when you bring your needle out of the top of a bead, don't immediately string on the next edging bead and go back down through the back. Instead, string on your dangle sequence, pivot on the last bead, go back through everything and push the needle through from back to front. I used a sequence of (2sb, bb, 2sb,bb, 2sb, bb, 2sb, bb, 2sb, pearl, sb). That makes a lovely long graceful dangle but a *really long* diagram, so let's pretend the stringing sequence is a little bit shorter – say, (2sb, bb, 2sb, pearl, sb). That'll make a stitch that looks like the diagram on the left.

Now string on another edge bead, bring the needle down and pass from back to front of the Ultrasuede edge and go back through the new bead. ...and you're ready to string on the next dangle.

After working around the tail section, tie off the thread and used the same thread and beads to edge the head section. While edging the head you may want to add an occasional dangle to make the "hair" look fuller.

The silver-lined pink beads used for the arms and torso were *very* pink. I wanted to tone them down a bit and help the color merge with the greens in the figure. Transparent lavender seed beads with a blue core made a good toning edge for this part of the figure. On the underside of each arm add a graduated fringe in the colors of the edging beads; this one started at the outside with (2 sb, bugle, 2sb, crystal, sb), adding one seed bead each time until the dangle nearest the body was strung with (16 sb, bugle, 2 sb, crystal, sb).

What to do for a strap? Stringing larger beads on a stronger line such as Softflex would be one possibility; another would be to work a freeform peyote necklace going up from each arm of the mermaid. I decided to use an existing pattern, the "DNA strap" from <u>32 Beaded Cords, Chains, Straps, & Fringe</u> (see bibliography). This pattern, with beads of one color spiraling around another color, allowed me to integrate the principal edge beads – the green Delicas and the lavender/blue rocailles – in a single strap. If you want to get more adventurous, there are any number of strap patterns in the books and magazines listed in the bibliography.

<u>Side Closure</u>

With this necklace I wanted to use a slender silver-colored hook and ring. Those things get caught in the back of my hair, so I attached the ring to the back of one of the mermaid's arms and the hook to one end of the strap, and sewed the other end of the strap to her other arm.

Feather Stitch Beaded Box

This little round box is easy to assemble; besides basic beading supplies, you'll want about ½ yard of solid fabric (I used dark brown cotton velveteen), about ¼ yard of quilt batting, a shallow empty can or round paper-mache box for a base, and white glue or Aleen's Tacky Glue. You'll also need some stiff but easy-to-cut material to lend body to various pieces. An 8 ½" x 11" piece of sticky-backed felt or Fun Foam is ideal (don't use regular felt by itself, it's much too soft); failing that, cardboard or template plastic or the plastic sides of a milk carton will work.

I used a 6-oz. tuna can for my base, so measurements here are given for that size can, but I'll show how I worked them out so that you can calculate your own measurements for whatever size box you're using for a support.

Preparations

Start by tracing a circle around the base of your box. You'll be needing that as a template for various pieces later on, and it can be very frustrating trying to remember the measurements after you've covered up the box with batting and fabric. Also, measure the radius of the base (for those who haven't done geometry in some time, the radius is ½ the diameter and the diameter is the maximum distance across the circular base, ok?) and measure the height of the side and write those numbers down. R is the radius and H is the height of the side.

Batting

Set the box down on the batting and cut out a circle just slightly bigger than the base of the box. Cut out a strip of batting about ¾ inch wider than the height of the side and long enough to wrap around the box.

Smoosh some glue over the bottom of the box and press it down on the batting circle. Then apply glue to the side of the box and glue down the batting strip. The edges of the strip should protrude about ¼" past the bottom of the side and ½" past the top of the side, to cushion things a little – but this isn't rocket science; it isn't even carpentry. So don't get out a ruler and start measuring and suffering. Just make sure you've got a little bit of extra batting at the bottom and a nice dollop of extra batting at the top, ok?

Making the Base

For the tuna can box, you want a circle of fabric with a radius of approximately 6 $\frac{1}{4}$". Again, exact measurements aren't that important. The thickness of your batting and the thickness of your fabric are also considerations. I'd suggest starting with a base circle slightly larger than you think you'll need; if it's too big when you get to the gathering stage, you can pull out your gathering stitches, trim the circle by $\frac{1}{2}$ an inch or so, and start over.

If you are using a different size box, you get to do a little arithmetic. Remember those numbers you wrote down – R and H? Here's a formula for the radius of your base circle: 2R + 2H -1/2".

(If you *really* don't want to do arithmetic, then go buy a 6-oz can of tuna, dump the tuna fish into a nice plastic container or make tuna salad out of it or something, wash the box out and continue using the measurements I supply.)

Using a nice strong <u>double</u> thread, run big fat basting stitches all around the edge of your circular base, about $\frac{1}{4}$" in from the raw edge. Don't worry about the raw edge or the look of the stitches, all this is going to be covered up.

When you're through, put the batting-covered box in the middle of your circular base fabric, pull the basting stitches as tight as you can, and push the slightly open gathered circle down <u>into</u> the box. Voila! A nice box covered with generous folds of gathered fabric. Ok, the bottom of the inside is kind of messy, but we're going to fix that with the next step.

Remember that tracing of the box base that you did way back when? You want to cut a circle of some kind of support about $\frac{1}{2}$" <u>smaller</u> than the base, and a circle of fabric about 1" <u>larger</u> than the base. If you're using the tuna can, that means a cardboard circle with radius 1 1/8" and a fabric circle with radius 2 5/8". If you're using a different size box, you want a support circle with radius R – $\frac{1}{2}$" and a fabric circle with radius R + 1" . The support material can be any of those suggested; it doesn't need to be thick, so I'd recommend a piece of plastic here.

Run gathering stitches around this fabric circle, lay the support circle in the center of the circle, and gather the fabric – not quite so tight this time, you don't want to buckle the support. Just pull until the flip side of the support (the part that will show) is smoothly and evenly covered, and then tie off.

Now smear the <u>gathered</u> side of the fabric-covered circle with copious amounts of glue, smoosh it down over those messy gathers at the bottom of the box, weight the thing down and let it dry. A can of soda or a bottle of beer makes a good weighting device that should fit inside all but the tiniest of boxes.

Preparing the Lid

Once the glue is dry, turn your padded, covered box over onto some blank paper and trace lightly around the outside edge of the top with a pencil. This will give you a feel for how big around you want the lid to be; it should come out to the outer edge of the gathers. The exact size depends on what thickness of batting you used and what kind of fabric you're using. For my box, with who-knows-what batting pulled out of the scrap bag and cotton velveteen fabric, I needed a lid about 3" in diameter.

Now here you want two support pieces with some authority to them, and the sticky-backed felt is ideal. If all you've got is skinny cardboard or plastic, try glueing some regular felt to it before you cut these two pieces.

Lid Top Support should be approximately the size of the circle you traced on your paper; Lid Interior Support should be the same size as the support piece you cut to cover the inside bottom of the box.

Lid Interior

If you're using the sticky backed felt, you can peel the paper backing off Lid Interior Support, stick it to the wrong side of a piece of your fabric where there's a generous border all around, and cut out a circle of fabric about ½" bigger than the support. (If you're using a non-sticky support, obviously, you'll have to glue it to the fabric before you start, or else trace around it and let that be your guideline for cutting. Do a line of big running stitches around the outside of your fabric circle, gather it tight around the support, tie off, and put this piece aside for a while; you won't need it until you're through beading the lid.

This piece will eventually be used to cover the raw edges on the underside of your beaded box top and to help keep the lid centered on the box. A thicker piece will be more useful for centering the lid but will also slightly reduce the available space inside the box (and if you're using the 6 oz. tuna can, there isn't much space in there to begin with). If do you want more depth and definition to your inner lid (I often do) then cut two or more pieces of sticky backed felt or other thick support, and cut the inner lid fabric a little bigger to make up for the extra thickness it has to cover.

Lid Top

For the top lid fabric, *don't adhere the support piece* yet. Just trace around it and cut out your fabric, a bit more generously this time; cut the edge of your circle at least an inch away from the edge of the support.

If you're using a relatively flimsy fabric, you may want to reinforce it before beading, either by bonding a support-sized piece of regular felt to it or by pressing on a support-sized circle of fusible interfacing. (See What to Bead On, in Chapter 1, for instructions on how to bond the felt.)

Now get some nice, thick, bright embroidery or cotton crochet thread in a color that contrasts well with your fabric and take a line of running stitches, *not* gathered, all around the traced line. You'll pull these out when you're through beading; until then, they'll mark the outer limits of the beadable area.

Beading the Lid

Thought we'd never get here, didn't you? Me too.

Working *within* the circle marked by your basting stitches, work four lines of feather stitch meeting at the center of the lid. I used flat iridescent peach sequins and silver-lined melon rocailles for this first set of stitches.

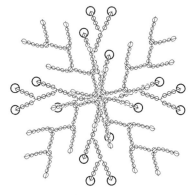

The second set of feather stitches was worked in SBT style, with matte copper seed beads. Size 8 iridescent matte copper seed beads were used at the points of the stitches and for the central bead in each stitch. The sequence for the first stitch in each group is (8/0 bead, 4sb, 8/0 bead, 4sb, 8/0 bead) and for subsequent stitches it is simply (4sb, 8/0 bead, 4sb, 8/0 bead).

For the last set of feather stitches I used iridized matte green triangle beads and matte green seed beads, with eight seed beads to the stitch, and TCT crossing – at least, that's the way each line of stitching started out. You don't want to take this diagram too seriously; as you work your way down towards the crowded center of the lid, strange things happen. You wind up using 6 beads instead of 8, or splitting the beads 5-3 or 6-2 to get extra length on one side where your beads have to curve over a previous stitch. Flexibility is key in this third layer of stitching!

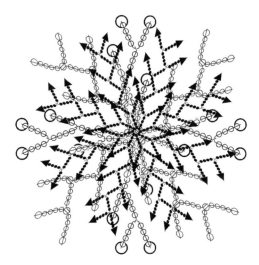

Assembling the box lid

Once the beadwork is complete, you can pull out the basting stitches. If you want a softly padded top lid with a slightly thickened edge, cut a circle of batting bigger than the top lid support but smaller than the top lid fabric, and put that between the beaded fabric and the support piece when you're assembling them. Attach your support to the batting or – if you're not using batting – to the back of the beaded circle, exactly within the guidelines you traced earlier. Make a line of running stitches around the outside edge of the circle and pull tightly to gather over the support, then tie off. Some of the support will be visible – don't worry; we'll take care of that in a minute.

Remember the piece called "Lid Interior" that you made way back before we started beading, then put aside in a safe place with the rest of the box? You did save it, didn't you? And you can find it now, can't you?
Good! Okay, take that piece and the lid top and put them wrong sides together, like this:

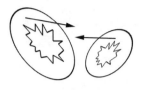

Now all you have to do is whipstitch them together and you have a nicely covered box lid. The inner piece not only covers the gathered top but also gives the lid a little depth so that it will sit nicely centered on top of the box.

Hybrid Rose Beaded Box

This box is made on exactly the same pattern as the Feather Stitch Beaded Box; the only thing different is the beadwork.

<u>Beading the Top</u>

I call these "Hybrid" roses because they use both methods of beaded rose construction; they start with a spiderweb construction in the center and end with overlapping straight stitch to fill out the outside petals. (See Chapter 15 for detailed instructions on the two rose stitches.)

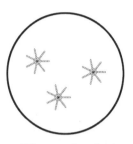

Make three 7-spoke spiderweb bases randomly spaced around the lid, using different colors of seed beads in each one. These should be relatively short bases. I used Delicas, building spokes from 6 to 8 beads long. With size 11 rocailles you might want to keep the spokes as short as 5 beads each.

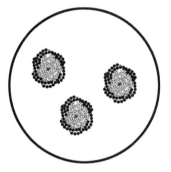

Work two rounds around each spiderweb using the same beads as were used for the spokes. Switch to a contrasting/coordinating color of beads and continue working rounds until you are nearly at the ends of the spokes. Switch to a third color of beads and work the outer petals with short overlapping straight stitches of 4 to 7 beads.

For the leaves, choose at least two colors of green beads. (I used three colors, so that I could get a different pair of greens with each rose.) Work four to six twisted chain stitches at the base of each rose. For each stitch, string six seed beads of one green and six of another. Be sure to twist so that the same color is on top each time.

Crazy Quilt Block

Original block pieced by Betty Robinson.

Betty's palette of deep, rich Victorian colors is not one that I would be likely to use, so it was a challenge and a pleasure to select beads that would fit the mood of this piece while contrasting sufficiently to show off both the beadwork and the underlying fabric. I'm not going to give instructions for constructing the basic fabric block here; you can find those in any number of quilting books and magazines. Let's just start with the embellishment stage.

<u>Preparation</u>

A single layer of silk or cotton fabric is too flimsy a surface to support most beadwork. The weight of the beads causes the thread to slide through the fabric, which makes it very difficult to keep an even tension. I began, therefore, by using Wonder Under to bond the wrong side of the crazy quilt square to a piece of muslin. (If you piece your crazy quilt block on a foundation square of muslin, of course, you won't need to bother with this step; two layers of cloth are usually enough to hold the beads.)

With any piece that may be incorporated into a larger work, it's necessary to establish clear boundaries so that you don't bead into the seam allowance. Here I basted a bright green cotton perle thread around the edge of the crazy quilt piece, about 3/8" in from the edge. It's easy to pull out the basting stitches afterwards, but I left them in so that you could see them in the scan of the finished piece.

<u>Beading</u>

A crazy quilt block is usually sewn from the inside out, but when it comes time to embellish the seams it's better to work from the outside in so as to avoid the problem of one line of beadwork trampling over another. Say you've got two seams, AB and CD, meeting like this:

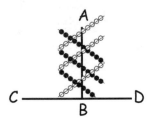

If you work the seam AB first and then work CD, you have two options, neither good.

You can stop the beadwork for CD when you get to the beadwork at AB and resume it on the other side, which can be a nuisance if you're working a compound stitch.

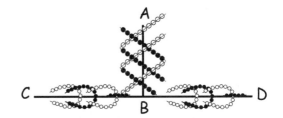

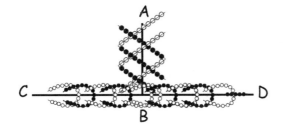

Or you can just bead over the previous work, creating an overlapping mess that blurs both patterns.

If, on the other hand, you do the beadwork over CD first, you can choose to begin the beading for AB above the CD beading, avoiding both problems.

About the Diagram and Stitches

Obviously, if you're making your own crazy quilt block, your seams aren't going to be in the same place as the seams in this block, and your colors and fabrics will be your own and will influence your choice of beads. The diagram on the next page, and the discussion of individual stitches after that, is not meant as a recipe to be followed exactly but rather as a key for you to use in several different ways.

If there's a stitch in the color picture that you particularly like, you can use the diagram to locate it and then find a discussion of exactly how that stitch was worked with what sort of beads.

It's also meant to be a sort of tutorial on how to embellish a crazy quilt block with beading: not just a list of the stitches used, but a brief explanation of my thinking on each seam: why I worked the seams in this order and what constraints influenced the choice of stitch (lots of ground to cover on one side but not the other, squinchy spaces to fill at the ends, etc.) So if you read through the list of stitches and use the key to refer back to the color picture, at the end you should have a pretty good idea how to choose bead embroidery stitches for any situation you may encounter.

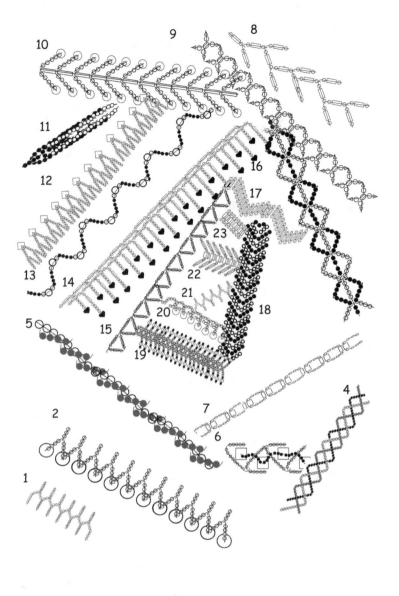

The stitches

1) There's not much room on this little corner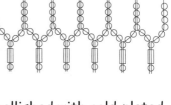
    seam, but I wanted a stitch that would reach
    out into the wide expanse of purple velvet. An
    asymmetrical Cretan stitch was the answer,
    worked in galvanized raspberry Delicas, with
    the outer points left plain and the inner points embellished with gold-plated
    bugle beads.

2) The seam on the other side of the purple strip
    presents a similar problem: I needed a stitch that
    would extend into the purple without obscuring the
    beautiful gold lace Betty had inserted into the seam.
    A line of sequin-loop fly stitch worked here, with very
    short anchor stitches (3 beads) just touching the
    lace. The light green holographic sequins stand out vividly; I paired them
    with dark green iridescent charlottes that almost blend in with the dark
    background, creating a sense of subtle richness.

3) After trying and ripping out a couple of heavier stitches, I realized that all
    the gold lace needed on this side was the lightest possible touch. The lace
    points are tacked down with individual matte blue seed beads.

4) Here's an example of three-color
    herringbone stitch in purple, galvanized
    pink, and iridescent gold. Notice how the
    number of beads per stitch decreases
    towards the end of the line, where it meets the basted border at an angle.
    It's often necessary to modify stitches to fit into specific spaces.

5) Whipped back stitch: a line of scarabee seed
    beads whipped with silver-lined salmon seed
    beads.

6) The base is a double chain stitch worked with purple seed beads and iridescent red bugles. It's threaded with more purple seed beads which hold down purple holographic sequins.

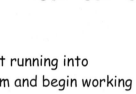

7) A chain stitch in SBT technique, using green 2-cuts with an iridescent gold cube bead in the center of each loop. The width of the cube bead forces the chain stitch to an open shape.

That's about as far as I can go on that side before I start running into intersecting seams, so now I start at another outside seam and begin working my way in again.

8) Feather stitch in TCT style, using twisted silver-lined green bugles and matte bronze seed beads.

9) A double fly stitch in SBT style. Each loop consists of the sequence (red size 8 bead, blue triangle, gold pearl, blue triangle, red 8) and alternate loops share the gold pearl, making a sort of X shape.

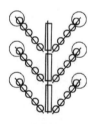

10) Fern stitch with matte purple bugle bead stems and bronze delica branches embellished with matte gold sequins. Because these particular bugle beads had rounded edges, it wasn't necessary to buffer them with seed beads. Note how the first branch of the fern stitch on the outer side is worked shorter thanthe other ones, to accommodate the beads of (9) which meet this seam at an angle.

11) Chain stitch in BCB style, with inside-out color change. The threading sequence for each loop is (5 red, 7 gold, 5 red).

12) Detached chain in TCT style, worked with each stitch perpendicular to the line of the seam, with the anchor stitch ending in a square red sequin. Pairs of stitches share the same sequin, giving the line of stitching a shape like a row of little houses with pointy roofs. Note how the last two loops are smaller than the others and are worked without anchor sequins, so that the line tapers to meet the basted border.

13) Serpentine backstitch with mixed beads. The threading sequence is (4 green charlottes, bronze seed bead, red size 8, bronze seed bead).

14) Two rows of TCT buttonhole stitch in scarabee seed beads and gold plated bugles, with tiny gold colored heart dangles, one row overlapping the other. The first row is worked with bugle beads in both stem and branch sections. Because the branches of the second row have to curve up and over the stem of the first row, they are worked in seed beads.

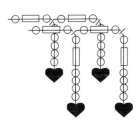

15) Closed buttonhole stitch worked with silver-lined orange seed beads and matte purple bugles.

Again, as I work towards the center, I start to encounter intersecting seams, so it's time to move out again.

16) Reverse braided fly stitch with galvanized pink and matte bronze seed beads. Note how the last few stitches are worked asymmetrically, with the branches on the right hand side decreasing in length as this row of stitching runs into (9) at an angle.

17) Serpentine satin stitch line composed with iridescent amethyst seed beads buffering silver-lined orange-red bugles. These are poor quality bugle beads, prone to fading and with very sharp edges, but I need the orange-toned red to contrast with the burgundy red of the large triangular fabric patch, so I put up with the uneven size and color.

18) Broad-line fishbone stitch, alternating iridescent gold cut 12's with green charlottes. Note how the line of stitching is finished asymmetrically, with left branches continuing beyond the right branches, to bring the whole line snug against (7) where the seams intersect at an angle.

19) Vandyke stitch in iridescent raspberry seed beads, tipped with bronze seed beads and red size 8's.

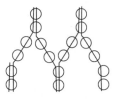

20) BCB buttonhole stitch win galvanized raspberry Delicas, with purple holographic sequins at the ends of the branches.

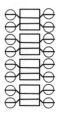

21) Cretan stitch in TCT style, using silver-lined amethyst beads, with 6 beads per stitch. It's getting crowded as I move towards the center of the square; there's only room to take a few stitches.

22) Fly stitch in SBT style, using gold iris cut 12's, scarabee bugles, and a gold iris cube bead in the center of each loop. The first two stitches are worked without the bugle beads to fit up against the beadwork of (15).

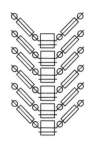

23) Double satin stitch (two "lines" of seed beads through each size 8 bead) with iridescent light purple seed beads and matte silver-lined yellow size 8 beads.

Hands Wallhanging

This is a quick and easy way to make a decorative sampler of some of your new bead embroidery stitches. To start, you will want two pieces of cotton fabric, about 15" x 15"; a piece of quilt batting the same size (dark batting is good if you can find it); a white chalk pencil or similar erasable marking tool; and 1/8 yard of bright cotton fabric for the binding. I used black fabrics to get maximum contrast between the beadwork and the background, but any solid color will do as long as you have enough contrasting beads to work all the stitches.

Marking the top

This will be easier to do if you stabilize your top fabric by ironing the wrong side to a piece of freezer paper, which you can peel off after marking and before quilting. Iron-on interfacing will also stabilize the fabric, but this will give you another layer to stitch through when beading.

After stabilizing the fabric, lay each hand down on it and trace around your hand with the marking pencil.

Quilting

Make a "sandwich" for quilting: backing fabric, wrong side up; then batting; then top fabric, right side up. You can baste the pieces together with thread, hold them together with safety pins, or use a temporary spray adhesive like 505 to keep them from shifting during the quilting process.

Set your sewing machine for free-motion quilting (stitch length 0, feed dogs down, using a darning foot). Use a thread that matches the fabric color in the bobbin and a contrasting, decorative thread on top. Quilt all around the hand outlines with small freeform circles, so that everything except the hands is held down with decorative thread. At this stage the hands should stand out and look kind of puffy.

After quilting, trim the piece so that all edges are straight and meet at right angles. (This is why we started with a bigger piece of fabric than you actually needed to hold the tracings of the hands; quilting shrinks the piece somewhat, and also may make the edges irregular so that you have to do some trimming at this point.) You can trim more than absolutely necessary at this point; the main thing is to leave the unquilted hands nicely centered and framed with at least an inch of quilted fabric on each side.

Binding

Cut your colorful binding fabric into strips 2" wide. Stitch them together at the

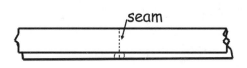

ends to make one long strip; press seams open, fold the binding strip in half lengthwise and press along the fold. You should have a long strip that looks like this.

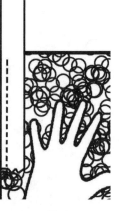

Fold over about $\frac{1}{2}$" at one end of the strip and lay it along one edge of the quilted and trimmed piece, like this. Stitch $\frac{1}{4}$ " in from the edge of the quilted piece until you are within $\frac{1}{4}$" of the next edge, as shown by the dotted line.

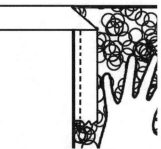

Now fold the binding diagonally so that it is parallel to the second edge and extending out away from the woll hanging. If you're not used to doing mitred bindings, you might want to stick a pin in the fold to hold it in place.

Next fold the binding back on itself so that the raw edges line up with the second edge of the hanging, and resume sewing $\frac{1}{4}$" in from the first edge, like this:

Continue sewing and folding until you have covered all four raw
edges of the hanging. Snip off any excess binding. Fold the
binding strip over the raw edge of the hanging and whip-stitch it
onto the back of the quilt. If your stitching was perfectly
accurate and you're lucky, the binding at each corner will
automatically fold into a neat mitre in front – that means it'll
look like this. If it's not quite so neat, it's legal to take a couple
of small, sneaky stitches to hold it in place.

Beading

For each hand, begin by drawing a chalk circle that separates the palms from the
fingers. You will fill the circle with a mandala form and use a different linear bead
embroidery stitch on each finger. Below are the stitches and colors that I used,
but you don't have to copy these exactly; I would encourage you to look through the
book and pick out your favorite stitches to show off, especially on the fingers.

*[Tip: You will bury your knots between layers of fabric, in the batting, as described
for the Pocket Doll project, above. For a neat-looking back, use a thread that
matches the color of the fabric. For an extremely neat-looking back, make all
stitches with your needle going through the top fabric and batting only, never
piercing the backing.]*

Note on bead selection: You want beads that will contrast well with the background
fabric. In general this means opaque or metallic-lined beads; transparent beads will
blend in with whatever's behind them and will seem to disappear altogether over a
dark or matching fabric. I used galvanized and silver-lined beads here to make a
glitzy piece; you could get a completely different effect using bright colored
opaque beads such as are common in Native American beadwork.

Outlining: Before doing any other beading, I worked all the way around the chalked
outines of the hands in backstitch, using a mix of metallic Delicas that almost
blended with the background (which, as you remember, was heavily quilted in
metallic thread). This was more to give me a firm edge that wouldn't disappear while
working than to visually outline the hands; they're going to show up clearly enough
when all the beads and sequins are on.

The stitches

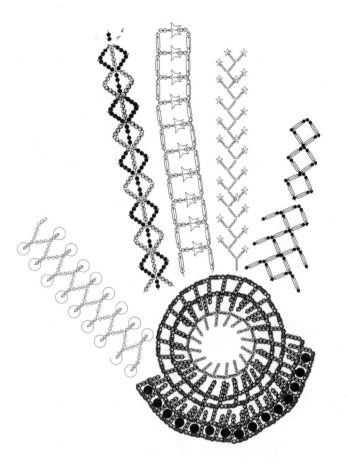

Right hand, palm: I began with a small buttonhole circle in the center of the palm, SBT technique, using iridized bronze size 12 2-cut seed beads for the base of the buttonhole and iridized bronze hex cut bugle beads, buffered with seed beads, for the stems. All the stems pointed inwards to make a wheel shape.

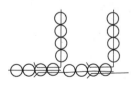

The next round used the same stitch with different and slightly larger beads: 4 gold size 11 beads in base and 4 more in stem, with the stems pointing inward to end at the outside of the first round.

Third round, same stitch, using bronze size 11 beads and matte bronze bugles buffered with seed beads.

For the fourth round I went back to the gold size 11 beads. Still using the buttonhole SBT stitch, I used 4 gold size 11 beads in the base of each stitch but 6 in the stem, and laid the stems up and over the bronze base stitches of the third round to create some interesting testure.

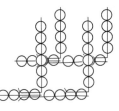

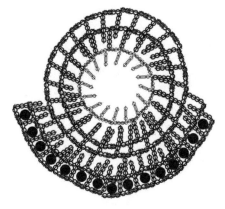

Now, since the palm of the hand isn't really a circle, there was still some space to fill at the heel of the hand. I worked crescents, rather than rounds, of overlapping buttonhole stitch, first with the bronze 12's and then with the gold 11's.

The tiny spaces between the stems of the last crescent were filled with 3mm cupped gold sequins.

Right hand, thumb: Cretan stitch, SBT, using iridized gold cut seed beads and ending each point with a small aqua sequin. The number of beads per stitch varied with the width of the area to be filled, from 5 at the tip of the thumb to 15 at the base. If you look closely, you'll see that I had to add one short stitch at the base to fill in between the thumb and the palm circle.

2-

Right hand, index finger: Reverse braid fly stitch, using galvanized green and pink seed beads.

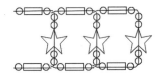

Right hand, middle finger: Open chain stitch, TCT technique, using silver-lined blue bugles, silver-lined purple seed beads, and matte iridized blue stars; the stringing sequence for each stitch is (sb, bb, 3sb, star, 3sb, bb, sb).

Right hand, ring finger: Feather stitch, TCT, using silver-lined red beads and tipping each stitch with a star-shaped sequin.

Right hand, little finger: Improvised fly stitch variation using silver-lined pale green bugles and copper-lined seed beads shared between stitches. The actual stitching is much less neat and regular than the diagram. Like the feather stitch on the mermaid's tail, it just has to be worked to fit the space available, and going back in to open areas to add stitches is very much a possibility. I had to get pretty creative to cover the changes in width between the base and the tip of the little finger.

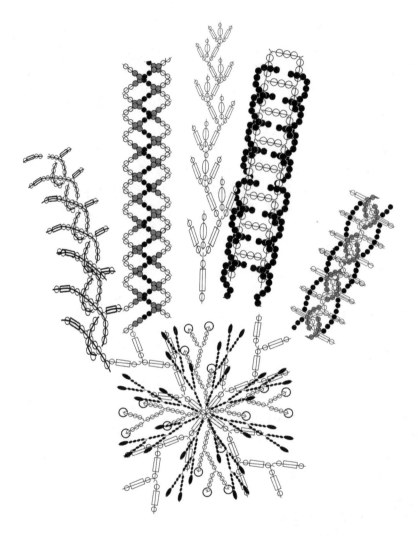

Left hand, palm: Feather stitch (TCT) worked in mandala form with overlapping stitches and with sequins or decorative beads accenting the points.

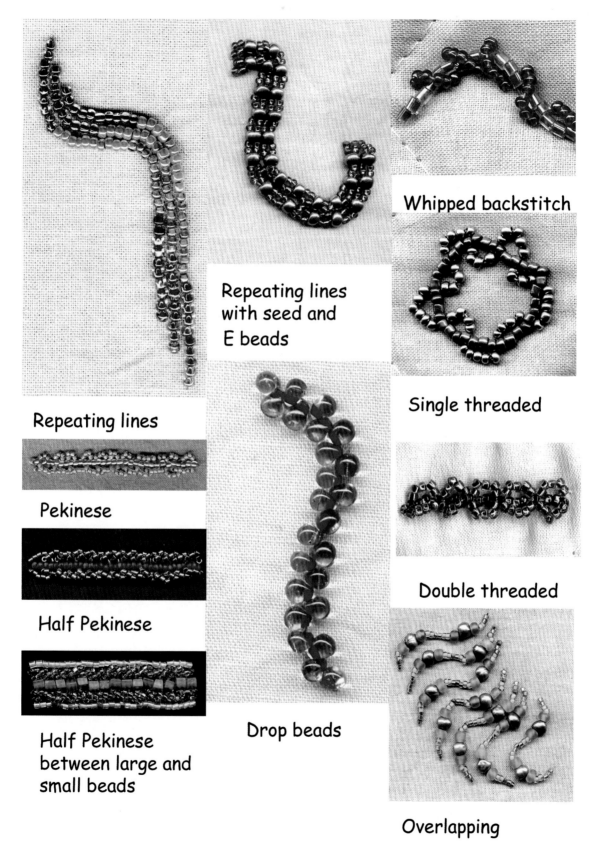

Whipped backstitch

Repeating lines
with seed and
E beads

Single threaded

Repeating lines

Pekinese

Double threaded

Half Pekinese

Half Pekinese
between large and
small beads

Drop beads

Overlapping

BUTTONHOLE STITCH EXAMPLES

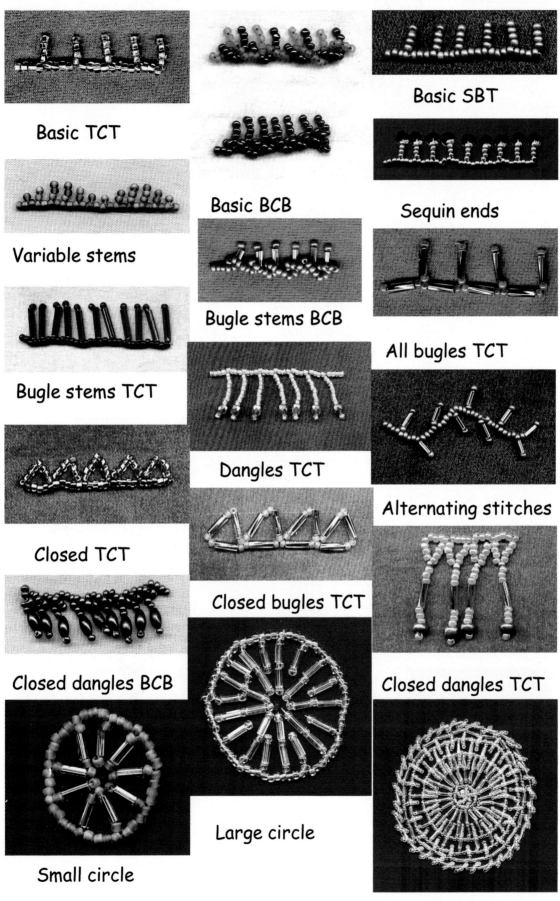

Basic TCT

Basic BCB

Basic SBT

Sequin ends

Variable stems

Bugle stems BCB

Bugle stems TCT

All bugles TCT

Dangles TCT

Alternating stitches

Closed TCT

Closed bugles TCT

Closed dangles BCB

Closed dangles TCT

Small circle

Large circle

Mandala

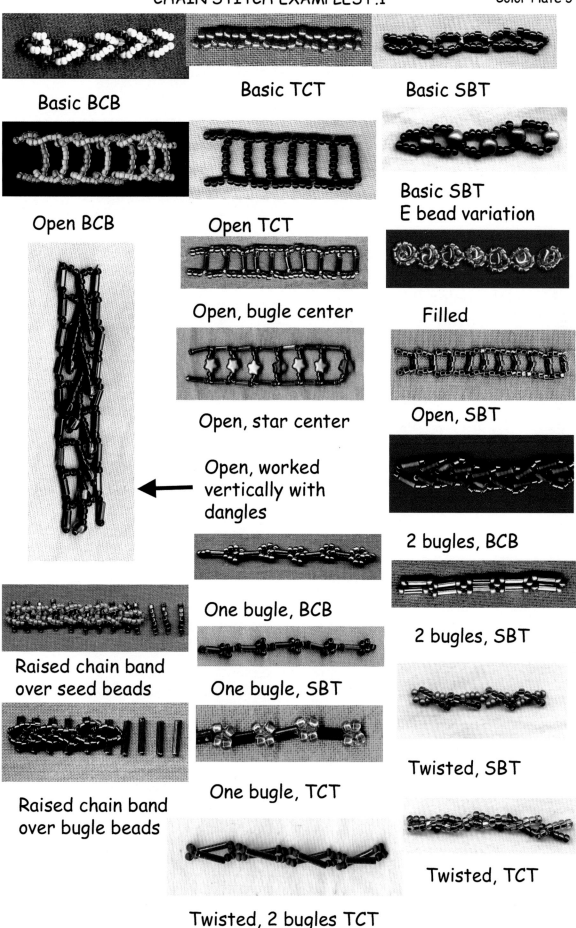

Basic BCB

Basic TCT

Basic SBT

Open BCB

Open TCT

Basic SBT
E bead variation

Open, bugle center

Filled

Open, star center

Open, SBT

Open, worked
vertically with
dangles

2 bugles, BCB

One bugle, BCB

2 bugles, SBT

Raised chain band
over seed beads

One bugle, SBT

Raised chain band
over bugle beads

One bugle, TCT

Twisted, SBT

Twisted, TCT

Twisted, 2 bugles TCT

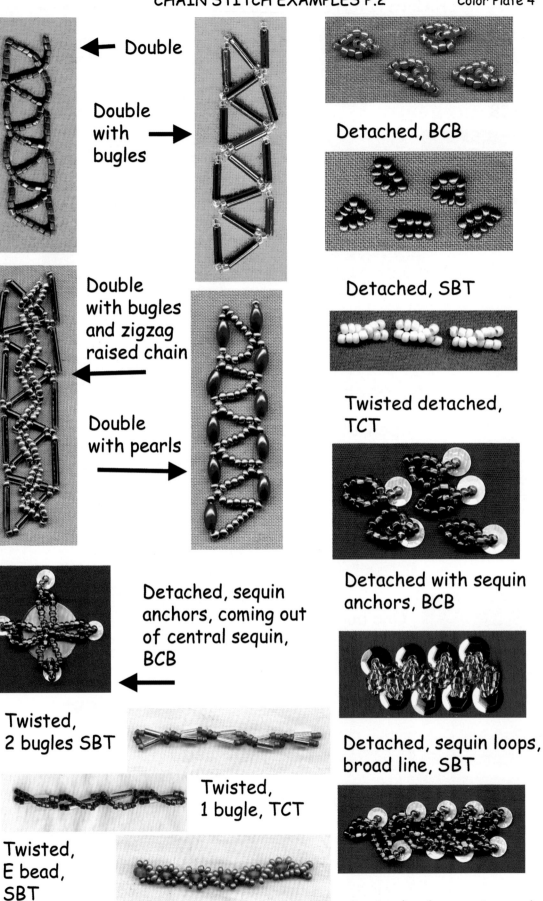

Double

Double with bugles

Detached, BCB

Double with bugles and zigzag raised chain

Detached, SBT

Double with pearls

Twisted detached, TCT

Detached with sequin anchors, BCB

Detached, sequin anchors, coming out of central sequin, BCB

Twisted, 2 bugles SBT

Detached, sequin loops, broad line, SBT

Twisted, 1 bugle, TCT

Twisted, E bead, SBT

Detached, sequin anchors, broad line, BCB

Color pattern, stripe, BCB

Color pattern triple braid 1, BCB

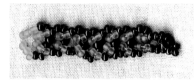

Color pattern, inside out, BCB

Color pattern, checkerboard, BCB

Color pattern triple braid 2, BCB

Color pattern, outside in, BCB

CHEVRON STITCH EXAMPLES

Basic chevron   TCT

Bugle diagonals TCT

Sequins

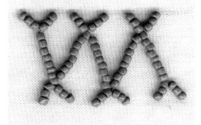

Fly stitch chevron

Fly stitch chevron with bugles

COUCHING EXAMPLE

CRETAN STITCH EXAMPLES

Color Plate 6

Basic BCB, one color

Basic TCT

Basic SBT

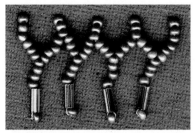

Basic BCB, two colors

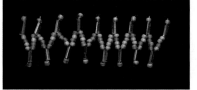

Sequin points SBT

Bugle bead points SBT

Bugle bead dangles SBT

Cube bead dangles SBT

Gradation within stitch SBT

Double threaded SBT

Gradation within stitch BCB

Gradation between stitches SBT

FEATHER STITCH EXAMPLES

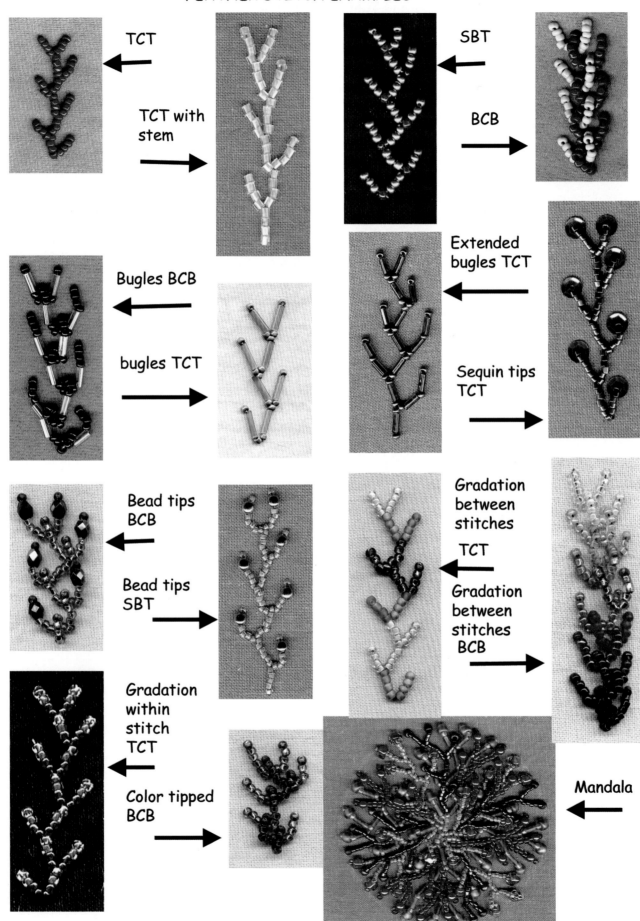

TCT

TCT with stem

SBT

BCB

Bugles BCB

bugles TCT

Extended bugles TCT

Sequin tips TCT

Bead tips BCB

Bead tips SBT

Gradation between stitches TCT

Gradation between stitches BCB

Gradation within stitch TCT

Color tipped BCB

Mandala

FERN STITCH EXAMPLES

Basic fern stitch

Close

Bugle branches

Close bugle branches

Extra-long bugle branches

Bugle stems and branches

Star sequin branch tips

Short dangles tapering towards bottom

Fern with detached chain

Longer dangles

Loop dangles

Value gradation

Closed shaped stitch

Open shaped stitch

FISHBONE STITCH EXAMPLES

Basic

Veined

Color tipped

Open

FLY STITCH EXAMPLES

Broad line

TCT

Bugles TCT

BCB

Bigles BCB

SBT

Bugles SBT

Anchor sequin TCT

Sequin loop TCT

Sequin loop and anchor TCT

Sequins and bugles TCT

Anchor sequin TCt
worked around
central sequin

Interlocking fly stitch
with bugle bead anchors

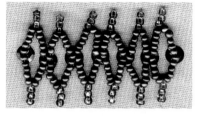

Double row of TCt
with shared loop sequins

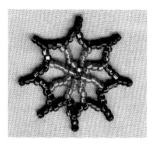

Interlocking fly stitch
circle with value gradation

Close fly
stitch SBT

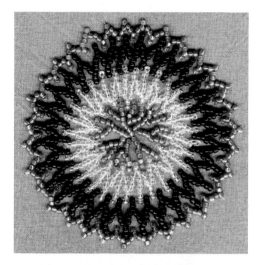

Interlocking fly stitch
mandala

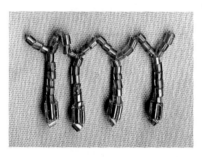

Dangle TCT

Close fly stitch
with bugles SBT

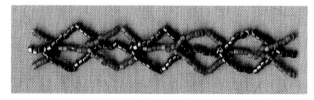

Fly stitch, reverse braid effect

Open herringbone

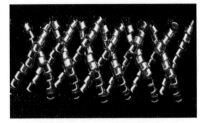

Closed herringbone

Sequin edging

Beaded edging

Whipped herringbone

Dangles

Internal stripe

Color series 1

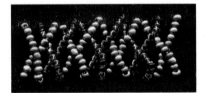

Color series II

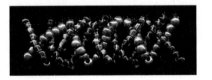

Three-color series

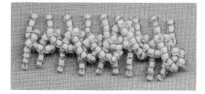

Basic stitch

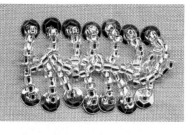

Sequins

Dangles

Bugles

VANDYKE STITCH EXAMPLES

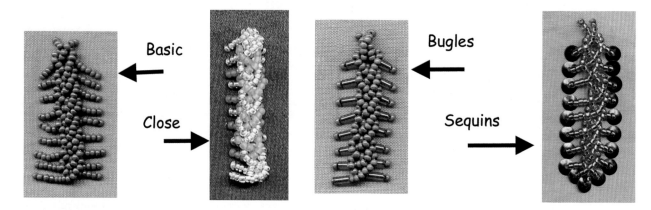

Basic

Close

Bugles

Sequins

ROSE STITCH EXAMPLES

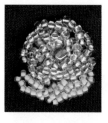

White spiderweb rose with central pink bead

Dangles

Classic rose with "leaves"

White center spiderweb rose

Spider rose worked with 5 values of pink and red

SATIN STITCH EXAMPLES

Shaded line

Bugle bead broad line

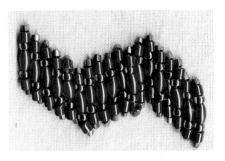

Textured line, staggered

Shaped filling

Shaped filling, bugles

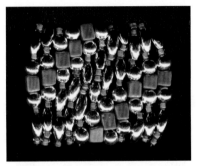

Textured line, cyclic

Shaded filling

Basket weave, 2 color bugles

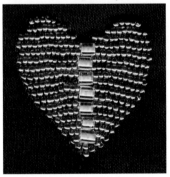

Shaped filling,
big center beads

Basket weave 2 colors,
seed beads and bugles

Basket weave,
same color
seed beads and bugles

Feather Stitch Box

Hybrid Rose Box

Mermaid Necklace

Color Plate 17

Hands
wall hanging

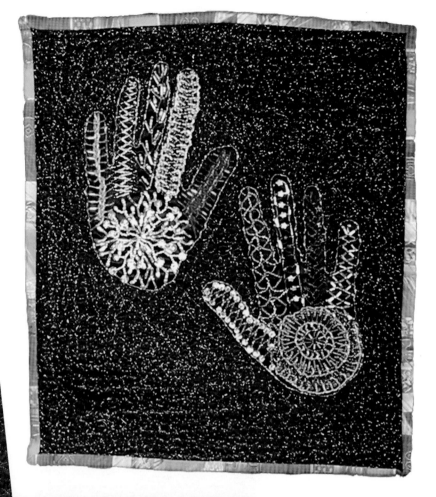

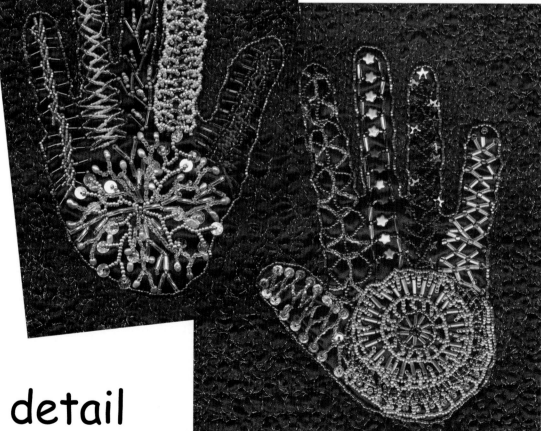

detail

Triptych

The first set of stitches used holographic silver sequins with matte silver seed beads.

[Tip: if you're planning to overlay stitches like this, put the sequin stitches down first. The sequins will lie flat against the fabric and the beads of later stitches will pass over them easily.]

The second set of four stitches used twisted silver-lined bugle beads with silver-lined seed beads. [If you want to use bugle beads, get those down next. Seed beads will go over bugle beads gracefully, but the reverse looks awkward and leaves bugle beads pointing up every which way.]

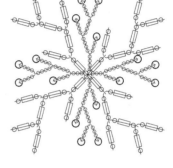

The last set of stitches used silvery pearls with clear dichroic seed beads. They weren't really black, as you can see from the color picture; I'm making them black in the diagram in the hope that it'll be a little more readable. This stitch set was worked eight times, between each pair of existing stitches, making a very rich, multi-layered mandala. Because I was working out from existing boundaries, rather than starting at the center and building circles outwards, I was able to fudge over the fact that the palm area isn't a true circle by working longer stitches towards the bottom – this isn't shown in the diagram but you may be able to pick it out in the color picture.

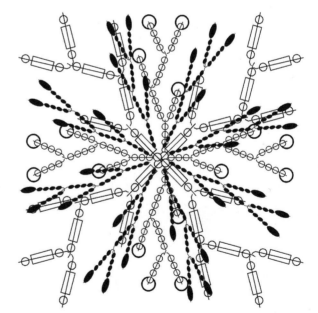

Left hand, thumb: A double stitch. Base stitch is Cretan, SBT, tipped with silver-lined orange bugle beads and center worked with matte orange seed beads. Over this are worked four lines of pseudo-weaving, two on each side, in pink and raspberry seed beads. (By pseudo-weaving I mean that the line of pink or raspberry beads appears to weave over and under the orange beads of the base stitch, but actually there aren't any beads on the "under" part – you just pass the needle through the top fabric under the orange beads and come up again to add another loop of pink or raspberry beads. It's just a series of small tight loops over alternate branches of the base stitch but gives a lovely woven look.)

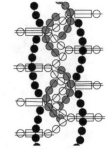

Left hand, index finger: Another double stitch. The base stitch, hardly visible in the picture, is a very open chain stitch, TCT style, using silver-lined lime green beads. The width of this chain stitch is less than the width of the finger, leaving room for a second stitch of BCB buttonhole on each side. This is worked with silver beads, stems overlapping the sides of the chain stitch and extending almost to the center of the finger.

Left hand, middle finger: Augmented feather stitch. The base stitch here was a TCT feather stitch with rainbow matte blue seed beads and silver-lined amethyst beads. This didn't fill out the finger adequately compared to the very rich stitching on the thumb and index finger, so I went back and inserted extra "branches" of blue seed beads and lavender baroque pearls inside each fork of the original feather stitch.

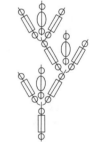

Left hand, ring finger: Herringbone stitch, internal stripe variation, in 3 shades of green.

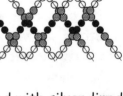

Left hand, little finger: Loop stitch, bugle points variation, tipped with silver-lined pink bugle beads and using silver-lined pink Delicas in the center.

Making and attaching a hanging sleeve

Now that your beaded work of art is complete, you want to hang it up so that other people can enjoy it. Here's the basic quilter's quick-and-dirty method of making and attaching a hanging sleeve:

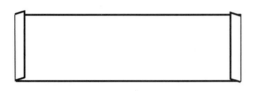

Cut a strip of fabric 6" wide and as long as your completed hanging is wide. Fabric that matches the backing is nice but not required.

Fold the short ends of the strip under by about $\frac{1}{2}$" and press in place.

Fold the pressed edge over again and press in place. Stitch down the center of each folded edge.

Fold the strip lengthwise so that the folded and stitched edges are on the inside.

Stitch along the long raw edge of the folded strip.

You've made a long narrow tube with smooth finished edges. Turn it inside out, press it flat, and you have the sleeve. Whipstitch the top and bottom edges of the sleeve to the back of the hanging. Now you can cut a dowel just slightly longer than the finished sleeve, insert it in the sleeve, attach a length of fishing line to each end of the dowel and hang your finished work like a picture.

Triptych: a work in progress

This is a free-style bead embroidery based on a wonderful computer-designed and printed background by Vernon Sims. Usually in open-style bead embroidery we try to pick colors that will contrast with the background and show off the stitches; here I decided to do the opposite, and use beads in similar colors to the background, so that they would intensify the flow of color rather than working against it.

The top section, shown here and in the color pictures, consists of circles and mandala forms created with some of the bead embroidery stitches and variations discussed in this book. I plan to fill the middle section with raised work and the bottom third with fringes, to illustrate stitches and techniques that will be discussed in the second volume.

Here is a key to the circles and stitches done so far:

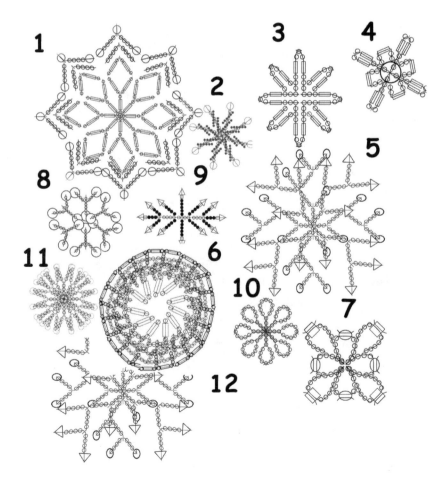

Circle 1: blue and amethyst

The inner circle consists of fly stitches using purplish-blue bugle and seed beads,
worked symmetrically in TCT style, with all the anchor stitches meeting at the center. The next round uses the same beads to work TCT fly stitches pointing outward, with no beads on the anchor stitch. This is followed by a round of similar stitches using dark amethyst seed beads. The outermost round repeats the TCT fly stitch pointing outward, using light amethyst seed beads, with an artificial pearl bead in the anchor stitch. The same artificial pearls are used at the beginning and end of each loop, so that the stringing sequence for the first loop is (prl, 8sb, prl); for subsequent loops you go back through the pearl of the previous loop and string (8sb, prl), and for the last loop, of course, you string just (8sb) and end by going through the first pearl of the first loop.

Circle 2: turquoise and red

 Short, straight backstitch lines radiating out from a central point are worked in silver-lined turquoise rocailles, ending with a red E bead. Each line of backstitched turquoise beads is whipped with galvanized red Delicas.

Circle 3: red and blue
Would you believe this is done with SBT detached chain stitch? The extra-long red bugle beads force the stitches into a stiff, rectangular shape that doesn't look much like the rounded curves we normally see with chain stitch. The first four stitches are arranged crosswise around a central point, with stringing sequence (3sb, bugle, 3sb, bugle, 3sb) and held down by stitching back through the middle seed bead. Four more stitches are worked inside the empty corners left by the first set, with the stringing sequence (sb, bugle, 3sb, bugle, sb).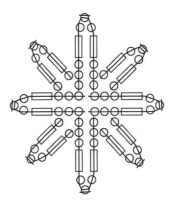

Circle 4: orange and peach

 The center of this small wheel is an iridescent peach sequin. Four modified detached chain stitches come out of the sequin, each with stringing sequence (3sb, bugle, 2sb, bugle). The needle is then passed back through the first three seed beads and the sequin, and the stitch is held down with a TCT stitch between the 2sb, which are at the top of the stitch now. This is a variation I didn't happen to cover in the Chain Stitch chapter, but the diagram should make it clear enough.

Circle 5: green and peach

Feather stitch working from the edge to the center of a circle. The first set of feather stitches were tipped with peach sequins and worked with green rocailles, TCT style. The second set, also TCT, were tipped with green/amber triangle beads and worked with transparent gold 2-cuts.

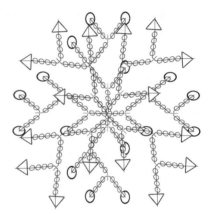

Circle 6: light green and yellow

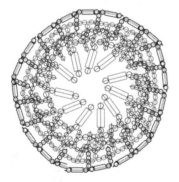 Several rounds of buttonhole stitch in various styles. The first round was worked in SBT with amethyst seed beads for the stem and green bugle beads framed by amethyst beads for the branches, with all the branches pointing in to the center. The second round, in BCB, used green rocailles, with the branches looping over the amethyst stems of the first round. The third round was worked in SBT with silver-lined yellow 2-cuts for the stems and transparent yellow rocailles for the branches; the branches cross over the green stems of the previous round in BCB style. The final round, also in SBT with branches crossing the previous round in BCB style, used pale green rocailles and silver-lined pale green bugle beads for the stems that form the outside edge of the circle, pale green rocailles alone for the branches.

Circle 7: orange and yellow

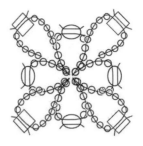

Two sets of detached chain stitches, SBT style, with large center beads. The first set comes out of the center for each stitch and uses orange seed beads, iridescent transparent yellow 2-cuts, and transparent 6/0 or E beads, in the stringing sequence (3 sb, 5 2-cuts, E bead, 5 2-cuts, 3 sb). The second set of stitches uses only orange seed beads and one iridescent transparent yellow cube bead for each stitch. Each stitch begins in the center of one stitch of the first set and ends in the center of the neighboring first-set stitch. The first and last sets of 4 seed beads in each stitch are shared. The stringing sequence for the first stitch is (8 sb, cube bead, 8 sb). The second stitch comes back through the last four seed beads of the previous stitch and you add on (4 sb, cube, 8 sb). Subsequent stitches use this sequence until the last stitch of the set, which ends by going back through the first four seed beads of the first stitch, so that you string only (4 sb, cube, 4 sb).

Circle 8: blue and green

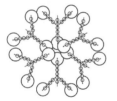

Sequin loop and anchor fly stitch worked in BCB style, using matte green sequins and matte blue beads for the loop, silver-lined green beads and the same matte green sequins for the anchor.

Oval 9: blue, green and copper

This is one of the few shapes that is not actually circular. After working the other stitches I had an oval space to fill here, so decided to work a double fern stitch (branches starting at each end) instead of working four fern stitches in a cross formation.

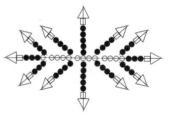

Circle 10: green and purple

Detached chain stitches worked in a circle radiating out from a common center point. I used a "lollipop" variation, SBT, very much like the one used for Circle 4, except that only seed beads were used here, to give a more rounded loop. The stringing sequence for each stitch is (3 green, 9 purple) and then you pass back through the 3 green stitches before bringing the needle back down at the center.

Circle 11: purple and mauve

A small circle of sequin-loop fly stitch, using 3mm cupped fuchsia sequins for the tips of the loops, purple seed beads for the loop, and mauve seed beads for the anchor. The "purple" loop beads actually have purple cores encased in transparent aqua glass; this gives this close-stitched wheel a lovely aqua shimmer in person, though it's probably not evident in the color picture.

Circle 12: pink and orange

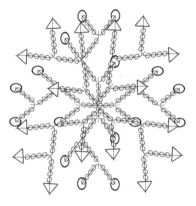

Another feather stitch mandala, this one incomplete where it intersects Circle 6. The first layer of feather stitches is worked in TCT fashion with holographic fuchsia sequins tipping the stitches and transparent orange beads for the loops; the second one uses size 6/0 orange-lined triangles encased in clear light green glass for the tips, and opaque orange beads for the loops.

Suppliers

There are many, many suppliers of beads, thread, foils and other goodies. The ones listed here are companies that I've had good experiences with. I'm sure many of the others are equally good.

Beads and Thread

About-Beads
www.about-beads.com

Beadcats
Box 2840
Wilsonville, ORegon
97070-2840
www.beadcats.com

Beadstuff
http://www.beadstuff.com/

Beadwrangler's Online Shop
www.7echoes.com

Equilter
www.equilter.com

Fire Mountain Gems
1 Fire Mountain Way
Grants Pass, OR 97526-2373
www.firemountaingems.com

Foxden Designs
12550 Sunflower
 Franksville, WI 53126
http://www.foxdendesigns.com/

General Bead
637 Minna Street
San Francisco, CA 94103
www.genbead.com

Shipwreck Beads
8560 Commerce Place Dr NE
Lacey, WA 98516
(360)754-2323
www.shipwreck.com

Sequins

Cartwright's Sequins
(web-only)
www.ccartwright.com

Plastic-Backed Foils

Meinke Toy
www.meinketoy.com

Polymer Clay Express
www.polymerclayexpress.com

Bibliography

Beadwork and Bead Embroidery

Atkins, Robin: <u>One Bead at a Time</u>, Tiger Press, 2000
Campbell, Jean: 32 Beaded Cords, Chains, Straps, & Fringe, Interweave Press, 2001
Clarke, Amy, and Robin Atkins: <u>Beaded Embellishment</u>, Interweave Press, 2002
Conner, Wendy Simpson: <u>The Beading on Fabric Book</u>, Interstellar Publishing, 1999
Conner, Wendy Simpson: <u>The Best Little Beading Book</u>, Interstellar Publishing, 1995
Cook, Jeannette, and Vicki Starr: <u>Beading With Peyote Stitch</u>, Interweave Press, 2000
Eha, Nancy: <u>Off the Beadin' Path</u>, Creative Visions, 1997
Thompson, Angela: <u>Embroidery with Beads</u>, Lacis, 1987
Wells, Carol Wilcox: <u>Creative Bead Weaving: A Contemporary Guide to Classic Off-Loom Stitches</u>, Lark Books, 1996

Embroidery Stitches

Enthoven, Jacqueline: <u>The Stitches of Creative Embroidery</u>, Reinhold, 1964
Howard, Constance: <u>The Constance Howard Book of Stitches</u>, Batsford, 1979
Montano, Judith Baker: <u>Elegant Stitches</u>, C&T Publishing, 1995
Nichols, Marion: <u>Encyclopedia of Embroidery Stitches</u>, Dover, 1974
Snook, Barbara: <u>Embroidery Stitches</u>, St. Martin's, 1963
Thomas, Mary: <u>Dictionary of Embroidery Stitches</u>, Morrow, 1935

Crazy Quilting

Michler, Marsha: <u>The Magic of Crazy Quilting</u>, Krause Publications, 2004
Montano, Judith Baker: <u>The Crazy Quilt Handbook</u>, C&T Publishing, 2001

Surface Design

Beaney, Jan, and Jean Littlejohn: <u>Stitch Magic</u>, Batsford, 1998
Grey, Maggie: <u>Raising the Surface</u>, Batsford, 2003
Hedley, Gwen: <u>Surfaces for Stitch</u>, Batsfor, 2000

These books are written for embroiderers, not for beaders, and they're not essential parts of a beader's reference library. What they offer a beader is wonderful eye candy and a host of unconventional techniques for preparing an interesting surface to do bead embroidery on. They can be difficult to find in the United States, but Deb Meinke (<u>www.meinketoy.com</u>) usually carries them.

Magazines

Bead and Button
PO Box 1612
Waukesha, WI 53187-1612
<u>www.beadandbutton.com</u>

Beadwork
Interweave Press, Inc.
201 East Fourth St.
Loveland, CO 80537-5655
<u>http://www.interweave.com/bead/bea</u>
<u>dwork_magazine/</u>

Lapidary Journal
60 Chestnut Avenue, Suite 201
Devon, PA 19333-1312 USA
<u>www.lapidaryjournal.com</u>

Quilting Arts
P.O. Box 685
Stow, MA 01775
<u>http://www.quiltingarts.com/</u>

Ornament
PO Box 2349
San Marcos CA 92079

Online Magazines and Informative Sites

About Beadwork
<u>http://beadwork.about.com/</u>

The Bead Bugle
<u>http://www.nfobase.com/</u>

Bead Fairies
<u>http://members.cox.net/sdsantan/be</u>
<u>adfairies.html</u>

Beadwrangler's Bead and Fiber Junction
<u>http://www.beadwrangler.com/</u>

CQMagOnline
"By crazy quilters for crazy quilters"
<u>http://cqmagonline.com/</u>

Bead Artists

Here I have to make the same disclaimer I did about supplies: there are many, many talented bead artists out there, far too many for me to

keep up with. This is just a list of
artists I know about whose work I
admire, who do bead embroidery,
and whose sites include some
wonderful and inspiring eye candy.

Robin Atkins
http://www.robinatkins.com/

Rebecca Brown
http://www.rbrown.co.nz/bead.cfm

Carol Dellinger
http://smokinonion.bravepages.com/
home1.htm

Nancy Eha
http://www.beadcreative.com/

Rebeckah Hodous
http://www.hodous.com/

Megan Noel
http://www.rdwarf.com/~mnoel/index.
html

Rebecca Roush
http://www.februaryseventh.com/Reb
/Welcome.htm

Mary Tafoya
http://home.flash.net/~mjtafoya/mary/
roadtrip.htm

Jo Wood
http://www.lakenet.com/~jwood/page
s/gallery1.html